**GRACE DE MORGAN** is a freelance writer, playwright and wine tragic. She has written for ATYP, *Good News Week*, Junkee, news.com.au, Playwriting Australia, SBS Life, Seizure, the *Sydney Morning Herald* and the Wheeler Centre. You can find her on Instagram @wineinaonesie.

# EVERYTHING HAPPENS FOR A RIESLING

## NOT SO FANCY-PANTS

### Your ∧ guide to wine

## Grace De Morgan

VINTAGE BOOKS

Australia

A Vintage Australia book
Published by Penguin Random House Australia Pty Ltd
Level 3, 100 Pacific Highway, North Sydney NSW 2060
penguin.com.au

Penguin
Random House
Australia

First published by Vintage Australia in 2018

Addresses for the Penguin Random House group of companies can be found at
global.penguinrandomhouse.com/offices.

 A catalogue record for this
book is available from the
National Library of Australia

ISBN 978 0 14378 8 850

Cover and internal illustrations by Cathie Glassby, Penguin Random House Pty Ltd
Cover and internal design by Adam Laszczuk, Penguin Random House Pty Ltd
Printed in China by RR Donnelly

# CONTENTS

# FOR IMOGEN, MY WINE BUDDY. I RAISE MY GLASS TO YOU.

*raises glass of red, spills it on self,
keeps smiling like nothing happened*

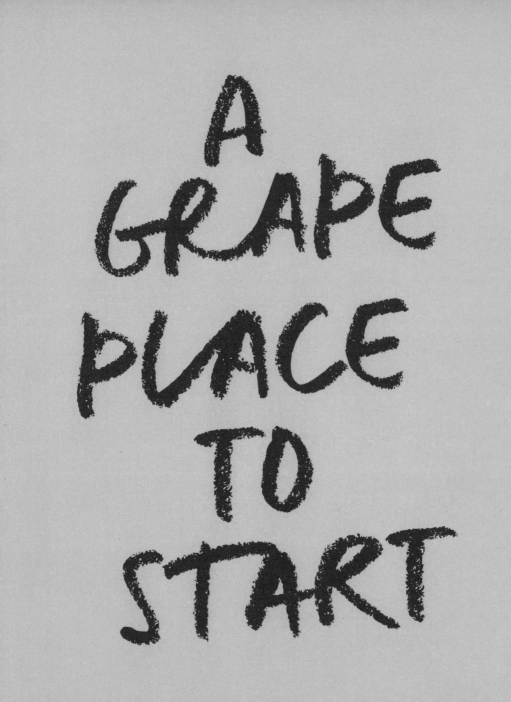

'I'VE BEEN WRITING
ABOUT WINE FOR
FORTY YEARS, BUT
EVERY DAY I LEARN
SOMETHING NEW.'

## Jancis Robinson

World-famous wine writer/
Owner of fabulous spectacles/
Actual wine expert

**WINE IS THE BEST**. The ACTUAL best. It's one of those little luxuries that makes your bath more sensual, your meal more moreish and your catch-up with mates that much more cackle-inducing. It's both a way to mark the end of a long day and kick off a freaky weekend. It helps commiserate and celebrate. The only problem with it is that there's just so much of the good stuff out there. So how do you see the wood for the trees? The vines for the grapes? The sheer quantity of info can be bloody intimidating.

This book is here to eaaaaase you into the world of wine. A way to decode and demystify some of the rules and rituals surrounding this delicious drank. A friendly push to get you to try new things and ask more questions.

Every wine lover is learning something new erry-time they take a sip. You cannot possibly learn everything about this nectar of the gods and call it a day. It's not a Rubik's cube. It's not the 'moderate' Sudoku from your Sunday paper. There's no way to get an A+ and a sparkly unicorn sticker. Wine is living, which means it's dynamic, which means it's essentially unknowable. Deep? Yeah, there's more where that came from, baby.

Don't feel pretentious – this book isn't about loading you up with obscure facts to pepper at a bougie white guy's dinner party. Sure, you'll learn about the history of wine, Aussie and NZ regions to watch out for, and what wines would be like if they were real people, but you'll also find out from the best (and most hilarious) about how to get more of the wine you like (without the wank). I've interviewed a variety of wine professionals and vino lovers who approach wine in very different ways, but who are all equally passionate about it. Think of them like a team of superheroes saving you from bad wine experiences and needless social anxiety.

# YOUR WINE WHiSPERERS

## Tim Watkins

Head Sommelier at Automata in Chippendale, Sydney
(Champagne Taittinger Sommelier of the Year 2017)

I started working in restaurants in 2000, but I didn't drink wine. I was a beer drinker and an occasional spirit drinker. I was actually studying music at the time. Like a lot of people who get into hospitality, I was only doing it for a year or two. This is my eighteenth year now.

**FAST FACT:** People have a real fear of sweetness, but some of the nicest wines I have ever drunk in my life are beautifully balanced Rieslings from Germany, which have an excellent sweetness and acidity to them.

# Amanda Yallop

Head Sommelier at Quay Restaurant in Circular Quay, Sydney
(Australia's Most Awarded Restaurant)

I fell into wine naturally by being a nerd. I think everybody's a nerd about something. You just have to embrace it. Growing up in Australia, I thought I was mature having a Kahlua and milk. I lived overseas for about ten years and when I was backpacking, I was buying whatever I could afford and whatever was on special. So I started experimenting and having fun that way.

**FAST FACT:** I've got girlfriends who've got the latest handbag, which I don't care about. Any bag I buy has to be able to take a magnum[1] and that's the only rule that I have. But their rule is the label. And that's fine. It would never occur to them to spend money on wine and it would never occur to me to spend that sort of money on handbags. Everybody has something that they're willing to spend money on once they've paid bills, students loans and everything else.

[1] **MAGNUM** = 1.5L bottle of wine

# Samantha Connew

## Award-Winning Winemaker at Stargazer Wine in Tasmania

I spent most of my childhood in Blenheim, Marlborough – the land of Sauvignon Blanc. But that was before the wine industry was really taking off and my parents weren't interested in wine at all. I literally remember the first time I bought wine in a bottle, not cask. It was Yalumba. I think it cost $7. Throughout uni while I was doing my law degree, I supported myself by working at restaurants. I knew that I didn't want to practise law and got hooked on this whole wine caper. So I ended up going back to uni and doing post-grad oenology and viticulture at Lincoln University, just outside of Christchurch.

**FAST FACT:** I think one of my favourite producers, in terms of Tasmanian wines, is Sinapius. He's doing a lot of really cool vineyard stuff and does a lot of work with different clones, whether it's Chardonnay or Pinot or what have you. Some interesting field blends as well. Down south, Anna Pooley and her husband Justin Bubb are making some great wines at Pooley Wines.

# Michael Ng

Winemaker at Ironcloud Wines in Geographe, Western Australia (One of Wine Companion's Top 10 Dark Horses of the Year 2018)

I grew up in Melbourne and first got into wine when I saw people drinking it with dinner in restaurants. My family never drank wine, only beer and spirits. I asked, 'Why aren't we drinking wine?' This was when I was about 15 years old. That was the start. Then I learned more about wine through magazines. *Winestate*, *Decanter*, *Selector* and *The Age Epicure* were my favourites.

**FAST FACT:** The best thing [about South West Australia] is that not just one or two varieties, but multiple varieties grow well and produce great wines, compared to many other regions in Australia and the rest of the world, where most of the regions have only one stand-out variety.

## Mikey Ellis

Head of Culture at Vinomofo in Melbourne
(Top Rated Online Wine Retailer)

I learned about wine by drinking it, asking questions and talking to people who know more about it than I do. I used to go out for dinner with my dad who knew a bit about wine. He'd bring a bottle, I'd buy dinner and we'd chat about the wine. I learned a lot about wine, but I learned more about him, which was beautiful. Wine is a great conduit for connection.

**FAST FACT:** We buy wine direct from producers and sell to our mofos online, which means we can sell wine at prices no one else can match. We only sell wines we love, and we taste a lot of wine – only 5% of what we taste we sell. And we do so without the bowties and BS often associated with wine. We're bringing wine back to the people!

## Becky Durham

Staff Member at Blackhearts & Sparrows (Melbourne-and-Canberra-Based Independent Wine Store) and Emerging Winemaker

I've always been around wine. My mum's parents established a winery called Willespie in Margaret River in the 70s (great Cabernets!). My dad came to Margaret River to make wine at Cape Mentelle. My siblings and I grew up tending (and trying to get out of tending) vineyards; wines and vines were a big part of our childhood. Later in life, I moved overseas and was inspired by Europe's rich wine and food culture. The next step was to come back to Australia and eventually create my own wine baby! Now I am the proud co-parent of L'uva Wines, a single barrique (225L) of 2017 Geelong Pinot Noir and an unreleased 2018 Blewitt Springs Grenache.

**FAST FACT:** I'm getting into Amaro. 'Amaro' is Italian for 'bitter' and bitters are my jam. Really great digestifs. There are a few, like Braulio. It's got a fruit core, but also a herbal, menthol edge to it. Fantastic. It is very, very good.

# Benjamin Law

Author of *The Family Law, Gaysia* and *Moral Panic 101*
and columnist for *Good Weekend*

I grew up in Queensland, on the Sunshine Coast, and because my
parents are migrants who didn't grow up with wine, my first experiences
were pretty democratic – cask of Coolabah or Fruity Lexia. During first-
year uni, the oesophagus was just a hole to put things in and so bargain-
bin Shiraz would go down it. It was not a classy introduction to the nectar
of the gods. Let's put it that way.

**FAST FACT:** I am less wedded to ideas of grapes and regions, and more
to what mood I am in and what I find delicious that evening. And it's a
one-off. Every wine in that situation is this delicious one-night stand that
you'll never encounter again.

# Rosie Waterland

Author of *Every Lie I Ever Told* and *The Anti-Cool Girl*

Year 12 formal after-party is about where my wine knowledge is at. That's where I peaked and stopped right there. I don't drink wine unless it has bubbles in it. I basically have the alcoholic tastes of a 15-year-old girl. If it tastes like sweet, bubbly fruit juice, I'm into it.

**FAST FACT:** My wine needs to be carbonated. I like a good Prosecco or Moscato. The sweeter ones. I've certainly evolved from Passion Pop. I probably now can taste the difference between a shitty sparkling and a good sparkling. And I can taste the difference between Champagne and sparkling. And I know there's a difference. So that's a positive. That's one thing I know.

A GRAPE PLACE TO START

## Mama De Morgz

My mum

My parents regularly had wine when I was growing up. My brother and I were given Port with water in it in a liqueur glass. We would have been seven, eight, nine. Not every night, just when they had wine. To go with the meal. We'd get half and half – Port and water. It wasn't a big deal.

**FAST FACT:** Sommeliers don't faze me. If they don't have what I want, I do ask for suggestions: 'This is what I like, these are the areas I like. Do you have anything on your list that's like that? What do you recommend?' And if they come out and say, 'This is a French one and it's $108,' I say, 'Can we do a bit better than that? I'm not that keen.' And nine times out of ten, they will come up with an alternative that's good.

# REMEMBER, WINE IS LARGELY SUBJECTIVE.

It's coloured by our experiences. Heck, it's coloured by our age and genetics. Nanna loves sweet, sweet Port because Nanna doesn't have as many tastebuds as she used to. And your mate may not like that tannin-packed[2] Nebbiolo you adore because she has the TAS2R38 taste receptor (making her more sensitive to bitter flavours) while you don't. This book isn't here to make you feel rubbish about your tastes. It's here to help you discover them.

This isn't meant to be a textbook. I'm not the golden-locked, girl-next-door teacher who's here to Eliza Doolittle you. I'm the wino in the attic who's watching *Bob's Burgers* on full volume, an above-average drinker who'll swap you Pinot Noir suggestions if you give me half your pad Thai. I like to imagine this as a light read on your weekend away, a treasure trove of trivia for your Tinder date, your second-favourite coffee table book. I haven't delved into extreme technical details because there are already so many great books out there that do it better. Also, my eyes tend to glaze over when people start talking about malolactic fermentation, soil types, and sulphur dioxide levels. And if you're anything like me, I suspect you feel the same. (Though skip to Chapter 6: Still Curious? at the end if you'd like more resources.)

Instead, *Everything Happens for a Riesling* is a tongue-in-cheek toolkit – focusing on Aussie and Kiwi wines, boutique over mass-produced, hilarity over heavy-handed descriptions. With that in mind, are you ready to get to know more about wine with me? Don't be shy. Let's get weird.

[2] **TANNIN** = naturally occurring compounds that come from the skins, stems and seeds of grapes. Often associated with that very dry sensation on your palate, much like that sensation you get when drinking a strong cup of tea.

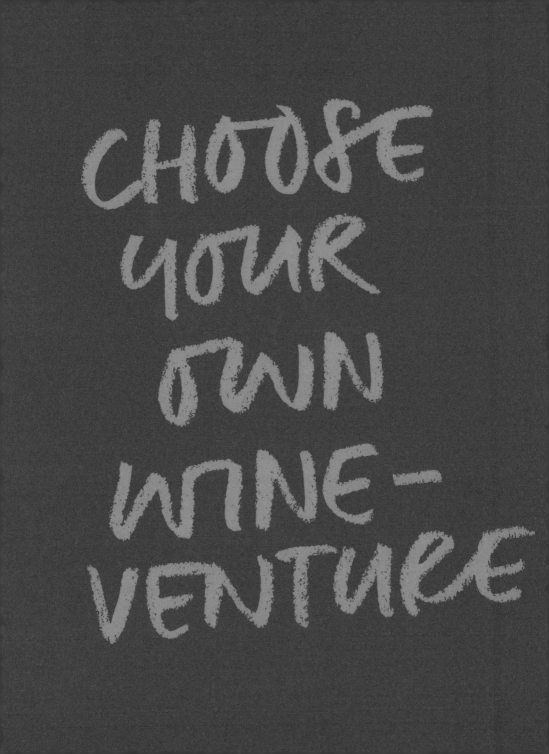

'I WOULD ALWAYS SUGGEST THAT YOU HAVE A WEDGE OF HARD CHEESE WHEN YOU'RE TRYING YOUR WINES AT HOME. THE PROTEIN IN THE CHEESE WILL HELP WITH ANY TANNIN.'

Amanda Yallop

CHOOSING THE RIGHT WINE is like skiing. It seems like a hobby designed for zippy rich kids, but it's actually a hella good time. It requires you to choose your own path and pray to god that you won't wake up with a broken arm. You can slide down the kiddie slope, cannonball over the moguls, or challenge yourself with a black run. Confused? Me too. Let's unpack that further.

Selecting your wine can be easy, middling or a bit more advanced. It all depends on how many questions you're willing to ask wine professionals and how interested you are in your vino. So – subject to how sociable and curious you're feeling – here are your safe (eyes down, no chat), adventurous (eyes darting around, some chat) and expert (eyeball to eyeball, all of the chat) options when choosing wine.

I've chatted to our crack team of experts about the five most common vino scenarios to make sure that you are COVERED whether you are at a bar, restaurant, bottle shop, family function or at home by yourself.

Don't be nervous – we are not going to let a few squashed grapes mess with your sense of self. You are the Indiana Jones of wine exploration. You are the wine god Bacchus with a few extra clothes on. You are mixing wine metaphors and not giving a James Halliday[1].

By the end of this chapter you will have so many tips and tricks up your sleeve, peeps will be all, 'Um, what's in your sleeve, mate?' And you will look back at them with tears in your eyes and an erection in yours pants saying, 'Confidence. All of the confidence.'

CHOOSE YOUR OWN WINE-VENTURE

---

[1] **JAMES HALLIDAY** = iconic Aussie wine critic.

# CHOOSING WINE AT A BAR

When you next find yourself in a bar with exposed bricks and a wine list causing sweat-inducing flashbacks to your high school French class – don't get anxious, get excited. Your wine adventure is about to BEGIN. <Air horns go off, someone yells 'Brap brap brap brap!' in the background>

## Safe option: *Go with what you know*

Don't be basic and choose the second least expensive drop. (I know, I know – it's the cheapest after the cheapest[2], but we are NOT going to let fear and indecision dictate our choices.) Plus, bars and restaurants know you're inclined to do this and aren't above pricing the wine they want to get rid of accordingly.

If you want to play it safe (in a bar or really anywhere TBH), try to remember the last kind of wine you had and liked. (Or alternatively, something you really disliked.) White? Red? Rosé? Sparkling? If you can remember some detail about it, say, what varietal it was or where it was from, you are killing it! There is nothing wrong with saying, 'Uhhhhh, do you have a Chardonnay? From central Victoria?'

---

[2] YouTube 'CollegeHumor Second Cheapest Wine'.

## Super happy fun task for winos

Let's resurrect that secret wine knowledge hiding in the back of your brain. Write down all the varieties and regions you remember.

_____

_____

_____

_____

_____

_____

(If this seems daunting, know that by the end of this book you'll have a bunch of references to draw from. Soon asking for a particular varietal, region or flavour profile will be easier than finding a reason why Trump shouldn't be president.)

## COME ON, GET APPY

Struggling to remember what wines you like? Take a happy snap of any bottle that you enjoy. Alternatively, apps like Vivino, CellarTracker or Delectable are a really great resource for compiling that data. And if you want to step it up a notch, start an Insta or Tumblr, so that you can share those experiences with others.

Genuinely can't remember? No problem. Try to put into words what flavours you're looking for. Something fruity or savoury? Something sweet or a little dry? You're not required to whip out any fancy-pants language. This isn't your Year 11 German oral exam. If your bartender is worth her salt, she'll connect you with the right wine (or at least something in the ballpark).

Also don't be afraid to name (or discreetly point to) your price range. Your bartender isn't there to embarrass you – quite the opposite. And if they do, they're being a muppet and you should take your business elsewhere.

When that glass of vino arrives, make sure to take some time to actually taste it. Have a good ol' sniff. This isn't a time trial. You've got all night, beb. Every glass of wine is a chance to learn about your own preferences. Even a bad experience is a learning opportunity. If the only thing you come away with is that citrus-y Sauvy Bs aren't really your jam, BANK THAT. That is some quality self-knowledge right there and all it costs is a moment of your time.

And if you're really feeling like a thirsty deer in the headlights, order a Pinot Grigio from Northern Italy. It's a light-bodied, zesty white that's known for being a refreshing crowd-pleaser. For an inoffensive red with a fairly neutral flavour profile, a cool-climate Aussie Tempranillo is your dude[3]. It's low in acid and sugar content. Plus, its soft tannins and savoury quality means it goes beautifully with most snacks.

---

[3]  At the moment, I'm into Jericho Tempranillo from Adelaide Hills and Born & Raised Tempranillo Nouvo from Heathcote.

**More adventurous choice:** *Channel your inner Kanye*

Now you're looking at the wine list and you want to branch out from your go-to Cab Sav. You're probably facing a long catalogue of wines detailing their producer, region, price and varietal (if it's a New World[4] wine). This is not the time to lose your nerve. Instead, lean into your ignorance like Yeezy. Be confident in your knowledge blind-spots. Own them like a badge of honour. Make an exxy clothing line inspired by aforementioned badge of honour. It's now time to boldly call your bartender over and get curious.

Make sure you sit at the bar, ask questions and try some samples[5]. This is the time to try that varietal you've never heard of (like my new beloved, Marsanne[6] – so savoury, so chewy). Alternatively, ask after that region you've heard about, but never had – 'Beaujolais? Is that the French region famous for the Gamay varietal? What's that like?' <Smash cut to you sampling an uber ripe Beauj and spinning around in a field like Maria from *The Sound of Music*>

CHOOSE
YOUR
OWN
WINE-
VENTURE

---

[4]   **NEW WORLD** = not European, post-15th century wine regions. N.B. this term is not indicative of quality, just history.

[5]   Remember, a tip never goes astray either.

[6]   **FAST FACT:** Oz has the oldest Marsanne holdings in the world at Tahbilk Winery in central Victoria.

### Expert: *Ask a wino*

When you want to make some advanced wine choices, go straight to the top and ask the professionals for their pearls of wisdom.

### Choose sparkles for celebrations

BECKY  Sparkles always feel like a special occasion. If you're feeling fancy, you can try Grower Champagne. Don't worry if you don't recognise the labels. Grower Champagne is crafted by the family, or the growers from the vineyards of one specific estate, as opposed to commercially made Champagnes, [which are] produced on a larger scale from fruit sourced from multiple vineyard sites. There are some great Cavas out there that are dry and finessed without a hefty price tag. There are some really playful Pét-Nats[7] out there, too, if you're up for something different.

### SRSLY though, keep an open mind

TIM  With every varietal that I've ever tasted, there are very good examples and some not very good examples. To write them off because of a bad experience is like sitting on a plane next to a loud, arrogant Italian and thinking, 'I hate Italians.'

---

[7]  Short for Pétillant Naturel. Really smashable 'natural' sparkling wines that are super textured and similar in style to a cloudy cider or beer.

### Aussie Chardonnay isn't your enemy

**SAM** A lot of people were drinking Chardonnay back in the day when they were horrible – alcoholic and oaky, the colour of butter. Just not pleasant. But wine-tasting is all about keeping an open mind and being open to new experiences. There are so many styles out there, and they've changed drastically over the last ten, fifteen years. Now Chardonnays are some of the best wines produced in Australia. If you write things off too hastily you're depriving yourself of a whole realm of experience.

My mum was the first person to introduce me to wine. So it would feel remiss to write a wine book and not include her. She's also just infinitely (and unintentionally) quotable. Meet my mother, Mama De Morgz.

### Mama De Morgz on having exxy wine on a date

**MDM** Say 'Oh wow, I like this one, but seriously that price? You got to be kidding me!' Then turn it into a conversation.

**ME** The waiters aren't going to mark it down for you, Mum.

**MDM** No, no, when you're talking to your date. Then the date might turn around and say, 'It's not an issue.' And you say, 'Okay!'

# TOP 3 ways to boost your wine knowledge

 **MIKEY** Taste, taste and taste some more. Taste everything you can! You don't have to drink it all, but taste it all. Go to tastings, get online and ask questions of winemakers, host your own wine-tastings. Get friends to bring a bottle of the same varietal, pour them blind, have fun with it as you compare. And don't take it too seriously. It's meant to be fun. Relax and don't worry about getting it wrong.

 **TIM** If you have a couple of days off, go to a wine region. If you're in Sydney, places like the Southern Highlands, Hunter Valley and Canberra are great. If you're down in Melbourne, you've got so many on your doorstep. You've got the Yarra Valley, you've got Mornington and Geelong. Also, Macedon is close. Do a day trip. I couldn't encourage it more. It brings a story into the wine that you're drinking, rather than picking it from a label or from someone telling you in a shop.

 **AMANDA** When you open a bottle of wine, the second glass will be different to the first glass because the wine's had time to open up. When you pour yourself a glass, take that moment to have a sniff. You automatically get pleasure. It costs you a moment of time and not an extra cent. I would do that every single time you have wine. You'll start to recognise certain characteristics about the wine on the nose.

## Wine professionals are elitist AF?

If you find talking to bartenders or sommeliers intimidating, you're not alone. Rosie gets it:

ROSIE  I would never do that. That's so scary. I could just imagine a sommelier being like, 'You don't belong here. If those are your preferences then get out.' I know that wouldn't actually happen, but because I'm socially inept and anxious all the time, I tend to look at the menu and just point at one. Maybe I would talk to them more if they recommended something incredible and I'd never tasted anything like it before. Maybe I just don't know what I'm missing. Maybe I think all wine tastes the same because I'm drinking all shit wine.

Rosie's not alone in that feeling. Lots of people love wine, but feel like it's a snob's game.

CHOOSE
YOUR
OWN
WINE-
VENTURE

25

BEN  I think people get intimidated by wine for reasons similar to why people get intimidated by opera. Because it's associated with class and status, it immediately feels exclusionary. There's so much bloody wine and you also know that there are some people – not all people – who are snobs about it. And you never want to fuck up around snobs. It's the same with opera. If I'm not enjoying it, is there something wrong with me? But of course the answer is, there's probably nothing wrong with you. You're probably watching a bad opera or you're drinking a bad wine.

If it's any comfort, Amanda swears wine professionals aren't judging you.

 **AMANDA** People think the wine industry is an elitist world. If anything, it's the opposite. The second you discover somebody's into wine or loves the idea, you're happy to talk about it. People in the wine world are happy for as many people as possible to come in.

# CHOOSING WINE AT A RESTAURANT

Restaurants are where vino truly shines. Food and wine are meant to go together, much like Jenny Slate and Chris Evans[8].

 **BECKY** If you think about it and pair the right wine, it will bring the meal to a completely new level. And some wines *need* food. Some wines you really shouldn't drink by themselves because there might be too much astringency. For example, a young Nebbiolo – you don't want to just sip on that on a sunny day. That's not really going to work out well for you. But for me, a triple cream brie, slow-cooked lamb shoulder or any kind of truffle dish are dreams come true with Nebbiolo.

[8] At the time of writing, they had broken up, but I live in hope, thanks to their adorable Twitter antics.

### Safe option: *Remember that asparagus sucks*

We've all heard that white wine goes with white meat, while red wine goes with red meat. But how about trying to pair weights, not colours, instead? Think: a light dish with a light (in colour) wine. For example, a goats' cheese omelette with a Kiwi Sauvignon Blanc or rosé. Or a big chunky hamburger with a full-bodied Shiraz. Too easy. My only strict advice: avoid pairing pricey bottles with asparagus or artichokes. These hateful veggies are the taste equivalent of tone-deaf. They make wine taste metallic, thanks to clash-y asparagusic acid (a type of organosulfur compound). So save that exxy Chablis for a dish more worthy of your affection.

### More adventurous choice: *Grows/goes together*

BECKY There's an adage: 'If it grows together, it goes together'. Pairing regional wines with dishes from the same area is usually a good place to start. You want to be able to taste the food while drinking the wine and taste the wine while eating the food - both complementing each other, without being overwhelmed.

More specifically, if you're heading to the local fish markets, Amanda has a suggestion.

AMANDA Take a bottle of Tasmanian sparkling or a Hunter Valley Semillon. Our weather is so great for moderate-bodied wines, particularly whites or lighter-bodied reds.

### Expert: *Vino-led meals*

Instead of matching wine to specific foods, why not try choosing
your bev first and seeing where that leads you? Say you've got a
hankering for a big, aromatic wine like a Gewürztraminer, some spicy
Indian cuisine would complement the fruit flavours, high alcohol
and low acidity really nicely. Or say you're sipping on a tannin-
packed red – for example, a young Cabernet Sauvignon – something
a bit chewy could match that flavour profile really well. Fatty pork
belly FTW. And if your sweet tooth is leading the way, how about
matching that Moscato or Port with something less saccharine, like a
platter of blue and washed rind cheeses. That way, your drink won't
taste thin and weirdly tart in comparison.

# DO WINE DESCRIPTIONS MATTER?

In short, nah. None (I repeat, NONE) of the wine professionals I talked to suggested you need a Rolodex of descriptors to get yourself quality wine. However, there are delicious advantages to having one or two key terms in your back pocket.

**MIKEY** Vocab helps, but it can be a distraction. You don't need to know how to read music to appreciate how it makes you feel and it's the same with wine. However, having vocabulary helps you identify what you like and don't like so you can refine your choices. It's a key and should be used as such, not to alienate and ostracise, but to empower and inform. The key terms to know are related to texture. I think it's more important to be able to describe how a wine feels rather than rattle off a shopping list of varietal characteristics.

**TIM** I find acidity is great to have in mind because acid is a vital part of putting structure into wine. Though when you mention the word 'acidity' to people, they really freak out. People think a wine with high acid is like biting into a lemon, but acidity is the feeling in the mouth around the wine. Wine with low acid can be clumsy and not very bright, not have any kind of resonance in the mouth. You can take a taste of it with no real feel to it, whereas a wine with good acidity is like drinking fresh juice. You can feel that acid in apple or orange juice, but it's also there in wine. And winemakers work really hard to get that balance of acid.

Here are some rad texture terms to help you get more of the wine you want.

**CREAMY:** Usually in reference to white or sparkling wines. Often to do with the use of lees (dead yeast), oak or malolactic conversion. In reds, you might ask for 'smooth' or 'silky' instead.

**CHEWY:** Wine that dries out the inside of your mouth, giving it an almost food-like quality. Not necessarily a bad thing!

**LEAN:** Wine that has good acidity, but isn't super fruity.

**OILY:** Usually a full-bodied vino, leaving a viscous-y feel in the mouth.

**OPULENT:** A rich, bold, big mama wine.

**VELVETY:** Wine that has texture that is oh so smooth and lush.

BECKY It would be so cool if everyone could come up with a couple of adjectives to describe what they like: 'I think I like mineral-y wines' or 'I think I like meaty wines'. Or 'I like something that's lighter and fruity' or 'Something that's a little bit more like a cuddle.' If people could do that, they would be a lot happier with the wines that they get.

**Super happy fun task for winos**

Prep for your next chat with a somm. List your preferred wine characteristics below:

_____

_____

_____

_____

_____

_____

# CHOOSING WINE AT
## A BOTTLE SHOP

You're about to get social with your buddies and you realise you're low on liquor. Maybe you're heading to a housewarming, maybe it's a dinner party, maybe it's a 12-hour _Real Housewives_ binge with your BFF. Whatever the case, go to your nearest retailer that isn't staffed by a gangly eighteen-year-old who refuses to make eye contact. Do not pass go. Do not collect $200. It's time for Wine-opoly.

## Safe option: *Option number three*

Okay, so you've got a wine-loving friend you need to buy a housewarming pressie for. Time to roll the dice and pick the first exxy drop you see, right? Wrong, compadre. (Unless you're minted. Then you do you, Gina Rinehart.) Price isn't always indicative of quality. I'm not saying make your way to the Passion Pop, but wine is just as subject to mark-ups as the rest of the retail sector. The same wine might cost three different prices depending on whether you're in Fremantle, Frenchs Forest or Frankston. Price is often heavily dependent on rent and employee salaries. So keep location in mind.

Also, a lot of pricey wines are intended for years of cellaring[9], so unless your mate has a wine cave stashed underground like Batman, it's probably best to buy them something that's ready to drink now. And if you're really looking to wow, get them something they wouldn't usually buy for themselves. Do they usually drink Kiwi Sauvy? Boom. An Austrian Grüner Veltliner for the win. Are they partial to an Argentinian Malbec? Bam. Here's a Barossa GSM from a boutique producer to knock their socks off. N.B. The best way to figure out what's same, same but different is to ask the sales assistant at the bottle shop. Use their sexy, alcohol-soaked brains to your advantage. Also the more you drink (with intention), the easier this skill will get.

(Or if you're feeling nervous about this whole gambit, just grab some celebratory bubbles. Sure, Krug or Dom Pérignon is your go-to if you're old money, but for the rest of us plebs, I'd be reaching for a dry Italian Prosecco or a cool-climate Tassie Sparkling.)

9   Cellaring is definitely something we should talk about though. Flick to page 47 for more info.

# MORE BOTTLE SHOP HACKS

- Avoid the bottles that are stored near heat sources or in direct sunlight, as this can mess with the wine.

MICHAEL  Wine is affected by temperature, which is why you should avoid wine that has been sitting in the sun, next to your stove, or on top of your fridge. Aromatics and lift[10] can be significantly affected by temperature. Taste as well. The warmer a wine, the more aromatic compounds are released. But being too warm can give the wine an [overly] alcoholic lift.

- Go to independent retailers for personalised recommendations.

BEN  People come to independent bookshops because they value the staff's opinion and I go to The Wine Society[11] in a similar spirit. I'll tell them specifically, 'I want a red and I want a white and I like these styles.' I know every bottle will be gold because they've literally tasted every single thing that's come through. They must be drunk as fuck. But as long as they're conscious and know how to operate the EFTPOS system – fine.

- If something's on special, ask why. It could be in rubbish condition, or too old 4 lyf.

[10]  **LIFT** = that refreshing sensation that comes from acidity. Without lift, a wine can feel flabby and meh in your mouth.

[11]  **THE WINE SOCIETY** = a boutique wine retailer in Ultimo, Sydney that specialises in independent producers and hard-to-nab labels. It also has an online store.

- If you're curious how others have rated the vino you're eyeing, whip out your wine app to find out. As previously mentioned – Delectable, Vivino and CellarTracker are good apps to start with.

# BANGER TIPS WHEN BUYING CHEAPER WINES

- Younger vintages are a safer choice for cheaper white and pink wines. Mainly because they are meant to be drunk young and haven't been aged for eons already.

 AMANDA If you go to a bottle shop, the best wines you'll find under $20 will be a Riesling or a Semillon. You can get something amazing for $12-$16.

## Today's best life hack comes from Rosie

 ROSIE I want to get bang for my buck when it comes down to number of drinks in the bottle. Wine bottles have that very useful picture of the glass with a number next to it. You've got to balance the cost of the bottle versus the number of little glasses on the back. So I always check that.

**More adventurous choice:** *Orange you glad we came over?*

'No, no, Gracie. This isn't a housewarming, it's a dinner party. I need something that a whole variety of people can drink.'

Ah, didn't realise that, mate. Why didn't you say so? Let's roll that dice again and move your tiny top hat across the proverbial board. This time, step into your bottle shop with your own tastes in mind. There are plenty of lifestyle articles that will suggest types of wine that aren't likely to offend anyone (e.g. light reds or crisp whites), but that's also a fast track to pleasing no one. So be a maverick and buy what you want to drink. Even though you are a special unique snowflake, there's a 90% chance someone else will share your tastes, making both you and other peeps very happy.

If you're feeling daring, blow things up with a bottle of orange wine. That is, a style of white wine made more like red wine, with greater grape skin contact. Half the crowd might hate the blast of sour apple some (not all!) orange wines have. But the other half might froth over its Warheads-candy-like qualities, leading to a chat about 90s nostalgia, circling back to a discussion about what the heck orange wine is (see pp 94-5), turning into a debate about sustainability, parrying into a symposium about climate change, segueing into how rubbish this government is, deep-diving into how rubbish the AMERICAN government is, hook-turning into Trump and LOLOLOL he's the worst and LOLOLOL I'm terrified LOLOLOL look at the time, I'm pleasantly tipsy, let's get our coats, hun.

CHOOSE YOUR OWN WINE-VENTURE

35

**TIM**  Orange wine has become quite popular now and people see it as new and trendy, but once upon a time that's how all wines would have been made because the skins help to preserve the wine. But we became so obsessed with clarity that now it feels weird if a white wine's got a bit of colour or is cloudy.

Wine has only been drunk in glass for a very short time in the history of wine consumption because it was always in a goblet or something dark, so you couldn't really see the wine. You only smelt and tasted it. They were the only two receptors you relied on. Now, you walk into a room of wine judges at wine shows and everyone is looking at it. But the smell and the flavour is really what I think you should take experience from. Whether it looks weird to you or not – it should really be about how it tastes.

*If you try a really sour orange or minimal intervention wine, it might be faulty.*

**AMANDA**  They could have been badly made or they could have been quite aggressive and had a lot of tannin. White wines in this world have a lot of tannin. But they shouldn't be sour or bitter. Everything is wrong about that.

*It's possible the winemakers skipped a step or two . . .*

**BECKY** They didn't do punch-downs and then it got heaps of VA (volatile acidity[12]).

Either way, remember to taste your wine with food.

**AMANDA** I would always suggest that you have a wedge of hard cheese when you're trying your wines at home. The protein in the cheese will help with any tannin.

So even though new things can be scary, it's worth giving orange wine a whirl.

**BEN** Last summer I had some orange wine and I was kind of into it. It's like a new sex act. It's painful at first, but now it's kind of okay.

### Expert: *Ask a wino*

Want to grab a super tasty bottle before you head over to your mates for some Netflix and swill? Bueno. Every wino needs their spirit guide – a boutique wine retailer who knows their shizz. Mine currently happens to be Blackhearts & Sparrows, a Melbourne-based, sibling-owned chain of independent wine stores who train their staff oh so well (and who seem to exclusively hire lovely people). I talk to local ~~legend~~ wino Becky about how best to select wine at your nearest indie retailer.

---

[12]  VA gives wine a vinegar-y flavour.

I want a nice wine – should I buy the one with the most award stickers on it?

 **BECKY** There are a few things to take into account when buying wines based on awards:
- Not every winemaker is going to enter their wine in every competition.
- An award demonstrates that this wine stood out in a room of wines, but maybe the more delicate, elegant wines were overlooked because of the sheer mass of wines tasted. And the attention-grabbing wines may be the bolder, richer styles. Imagine tasting 50+ red wines! For me personally, the punchiest, richest red wine would leave the more lasting impression.
- Whoever is judging the wine may not share your taste or palate preferences. If it has a shiny thing on it, some panel liked it, but that doesn't guarantee that you will.

Say I walk into your store and I'm looking for a wine, what would your usual process be in helping me find my perfect wine?

 **BECKY** I usually first ask, 'Do you want a red, a white or a rosé?' so I can understand what kind of wine they're in the mood for. There are increasingly more people going for orange or natural wines now too, so another apt question

I'd ask pretty much straight-up is, 'Do you want something conventional or unconventional?'

Say it's a white wine: 'Do you want something light and crisp? Do you want something rich and textural?' I then narrow it down further because there are so many wines to choose from, and both you and I just want to make sure it's the right one! With reds, it's more, 'Do you want something light, medium or full-bodied?' And then I go in that direction and try to discern from that.

As a customer on a journey to finding your 'perfect wine/s', it helps to be mindful or take time to notice the different flavours in your mouth, the way it feels on your tongue. Or when you recognise if you do or don't like your wine, to ask yourself 'Why?'.

Price point is another thing to keep in mind. I always ask, 'How much would you like to spend or not spend?' Some people want to spend a little bit and have something special, or a bit more of an experience, other people want something cheap and cheerful, more weekday winner wines.

Most wine retailers just want you to have a good experience, to have a happy time with your wine and to come back and have a bit of banter about what you liked or didn't like so we can find things that you will love!

Do you judge people when they tell you their price range?

BECKY Hell no. I just want them to be happy.

You won't get a bigger commision if you upsell?

BECKY We're not commission-based. We get jobs because we are passionate about wine or beers, but more so because we like people. We like people to be happy.

Is there any varietal you're really excited about at the moment?

BECKY Nerello Mascalese is my baby. I spent a little time in Sicily last year, which blew my mind! There are some incredible producers creating Etna Rosso (which is often a blend of Nerello Mascalese and Nerello Cappuccio) on the active volcano that is Mount Etna. The vineyards there are based on this incredibly rocky, volcanic soil so for me there is that sense of minerality and an ashy quality wrapped around a chewy, raspberry core. Keep an eye out for Fessina, iVigneri (Salvo Foti is an absolute dreamboat) and Passopisciaro. Yum.

**Buying wine for the pretty label is a bad idea?**

**BEN** The aesthetics tell me a bit about your value system as well. It's kind of shallow, but if I don't like your aesthetics I'm probably not going to like your wine. If you think that looks good, you probably think something terrible tastes good as well.

**BECKY** If you connect with a bottle of wine based on a label and if you have no preconceived expectations about what the wine tastes like – it's fine. If you have an idea about what kind of flavours you're feeling like or if you have a special dish you'd like to pair the wine with, then asking for a helping hand or reading the back label is going to be less of a roulette and more of a guaranteed good time.

CHOOSE
YOUR
OWN
WINE–
VENTURE

41

## CHOOSING WINE FOR YOUR FAMILY

Whether you're super tight with your big, high-fiving bro or wish Aunt Margot would stop trying to lure you into that pyramid scheme, family events can be tricky to navigate. We all have un-dealt-with shizz within our gene pool and things can bubble to the surface when alcohol grabs the reins. Let's take the time to figure out some strategies for combining wine and family.

### Safe option: *Low and slow*

Wine with low alcohol content is probably your safest option here, and you can check how much is in each bottle by looking at the back label. There'll be a percentage on it that indicates the amount of alcohol in the bottle (that is, a percentage known as the ABV or 'Alcohol By Volume'). Most table wines are about 13-15%. A sparkling tends to be around 12-13.5%, but will likely weasel its way into your bloodstream quicker, thanks to dem bubbles. That is, it won't necessarily get you drunker, but it will be absorbed faster, meaning you feel the effects more rapidly than wine sans gas.

Your most harmless option is probably a Moscato or Asti Spumante. The light fizz of these styles is both celebratory and Champagne-esque, however it has the distinct advantage of being lower in alcohol (most likely 5-9%). So your chances of outing your baby sister for pranging Dad's car (after she claimed someone backed into her at Woolies) are substantially lower and you will live to fight another day.

TRUE OR FALSE    **Box wine is no good?**

MIKEY It's good value if you're a student in a share house. Wine on tap is a good thing when you're going for quantity over quality. Having said that there is some good quality cask wine, but it's a last resort.

**SAM** Sulphur levels tend to be a lot higher in cask wine than in bottled wine. That has an impact on the aromatics and can make wine quite harsh on the palate. I'm sure, like everything in Australia, we'd be able to find a good one - there are probably some bargains to be had. It would be interesting to do a tasting with cask wines, actually.

## More adventurous choice: *Russian roulette*

If you really want to throw caution to the wind, go the opposite end of the spectrum and get very drunk very early and pass out in your nephew's cot. The warmer the climate of origin, the higher the alcohol content that wine is likely to have. High-octane wines that fit this bill include a Hunter Valley Chardonnay , a Barossa Valley Shiraz , a Chilean Malbec , or a fortified wine[13] from Rutherglen, Victoria.

(Last Christmas, I chose this route and hate-drank a bottle of McLaren Vale Shiraz and several nips of whisky on the first night of our family holiday. Safe to say, this led to me being very sick the next morning and very, very miserable. So I would advise the former low-alcohol strategy over the latter.)

CHOOSE
YOUR
OWN
WINE-
VENTURE

43

---

[13]   Careful with those fortified wines, though. They can range from 15-20% ABV i.e. getting closer to spirits territory.

# HANGOVER CURES

 **ROSIE** Two Panadol and try to drink a bottle of water before bed. It always helps if I'm in the right frame of mind to bless Future Rosie with that gift. If Present Rosie isn't smart enough to help out Future Rosie, then two Panadol as soon as I wake up, lots of water and a greasy, greasy, greasy breakfast. Eggs, sausages, bread. Lots of bread.

 **BEN** Miso soup. Bed rest. Water. Seriously, next time you're hung-over, have some miso soup. It's got salt, it's got probiotics, it's got living cultures. You'll feel so comforted. It won't cure your hangover, but it will really help.

 **BECKY** A swim in the ocean or, if that's out of the question, a cold shower will do. I also find that cuddles, meditation, a lot of sparkling mineral water, bacon, a beer and a nap all help.

**Expert:** *Ask a family member*

Talking to your family about their relationship to alcohol is actually a surprisingly rich topic that may unearth some pretty funny insights you've never heard before. I found this out firsthand when I sat down with my own mother to see if the apple doesn't fall far from the tipsy tree.

First up, Mum, how would you rate your wine knowledge?
Reasonable.

What varieties do you tend to gravitate towards?
If it's a red, it's a Pinot Noir. Or if it's a white, I like Semillon Sauvignon Blanc.

I feel like we're above-average drinkers. I've talked to a few people who don't drink at home — only socially — and I realise that in our family we definitely use it to wind down.
I think it's a cultural thing. If you grow up with wine, it's part of the norm. Some people have Weetbix for breakfast . . .

Some people have a pint of Guinness for breakfast.
Exactly! It's what you're used to.

So what is the best thing about wine?
Jesus turned water into wine, so there's got to be something there.

If you could have a wine with anyone in the world — past or present — who would it be?
George Clooney would be fine. With a Nespresso afterwards.

# WHICH FAMOUS PERSON WOULD YOU LOVE TO HAVE A WINE WITH?

 **ROSIE**  Gilda Radner. Season One, SNL. One of the greatest female comedians of our time. In a cosy bar with comfy seating and quiet music. Basically, my living room recreated in public.

 **BEN**  Oh, Jesus Christ, absolutely. I'd love to have a Chardonnay with him and get his thoughts on the gays. Considering he never said anything about us and spent a lot of his life hanging out with sex workers, I have this weird hunch he'd totally be okay with us. Also I really want to ask him about when he turned the water into wine. Which varietal was it?

 **SAM**  Helen Mirren. I think she would be a complete crack-up. She seems funny and intelligent. Bolshie as well.

And, as for me: Jennifer Lawrence. I like how self-deprecating she is and feel like we'd end up prank calling my Year Eight boyfriend or crashing a bar mitzvah.

# CHOOSING WINE FOR YOURSELF

Buying wine for yourself should be like dating done right: considered, playful and resulting in orgasms. Hear me out. The wine that you buy for yourself should welcome you home when you've had a rough day at work. It should sit with you while you're soaking in the tub blasting Enya's 'Orinoco Flow' un-ironically. This is the wine that opens you up to new tastes and sensations, despite the fact that you're cocooned in a little blankie watching an ep of *The Simpsons* you've already seen four times. It should be accessible, but also a treat. An accessible treat.

## Safe option: *Stock up and cellar right*

You should always have a glass of wine on offer for guests (and yourself). An easy way to do this is by buying a case of six or twelve bottles. If there's a winery with a particular vintage[13] and varietal you know you love, give them your credit card details on the immediate. Having a supply of vino at the ready is a really great life choice – a comfort that even if your day has been rubbish, your wine will never be. Just make sure you cellar those puppies right.

According to winemaker Michael Ng, cellaring wine is all about being patient and choosing the right varieties or styles of wine – for example, a Riesling over a Sauvignon Blanc (thanks to Riesling's strong acidity). His advice is to start small, in the coolest and most humid part of your house, 'I started my own cellar under the bathroom sink.' Alternatively you could stash your grog under the house or in a thermo-controlled fridge.

CHOOSE
YOUR
OWN
WINE-
VENTURE

47

---

[13] **VINTAGE** = the year in which the wine was harvested.
**NON-VINTAGE** = a blend of wines from different years.

# DO WINE GLASSES MATTER?

 **BECKY** Good glassware does make a difference. As an experiment, pour wine into both a water glass and a wine glass to taste and smell the difference. The size of the glass determines the surface area of the wine exposed to oxygen, which helps change the structure of the wine, break down the tannins and release aromas. In saying that, if you're more about the good time and less focused on the wine, a tumbler does the trick.

 **TIM** There are certain wines that really benefit from a bigger glass. All you need is a regular standard glass and a few that are a little bigger: one standard glass for while you're cooking your dinner, and one that you can pull out if you have a nice bottle and you want to open it up.

Pinot glasses will often be closed at the top because Pinots rely on aromatics – the closed top will increase their aromatic element. You'll find Cabernet and Chardonnay glasses will be more open as these wines don't rely as much on that aromatic element for their flavour profiles. The aromatics will still be there, but it's really about opening that wine.

## More adventurous choice: *Wine without clothes*

When you're choosing vino for your home, remember that wine goes through trends and trends can be fickle. Why not buck the fads and try something that hasn't been popular for a while, like Sherry or Merlot? Much like iconically bookish characters (cough Hermione Granger cough), unpopular wines often are undervalued and have spent a lot of time improving themselves while no one else is watching.

You can also consider buying a cleanskin to accompany your Tuesday night personal pizza party. This has been my fave option when I'm a) low on cashola, and b) happy to roll the dice with my wine.

'Wait,' you may say. 'You've jumped ahead. WTF is a cleanskin?' My bad. Let's circle back.

A cleanskin is an Antipodean term for a wine without a label. Cleanskins only list the varietal, vintage and sometimes the region, but not the winemaker or winery. This allows wineries to manage over-supply without undercutting their brand and prices. This practice started in the 2000s and means you can get brand-name wine without brand-name prices. The Kemeny's Hidden Label range is my go-to for cleanskins. You get high-quality, highly rated wines up to 50% off their usual price.

Not all cleanskins are winners, though. In fact, some are pretty dire cast-offs. Worst case scenario – they're a cheeky way to stock up on your cooking wine stash.

**HOT TIP:**

If you don't finish your bottle, pop it in the fridge (whether red or white) and it should last up to three days. And if you transfer it into a smaller bottle and cap it, it'll last even longer - the less oxygen the wine comes into contact with, the less chance it has to get oh so vinegary.

# WHAT'S THE DEAL WITH DECANTERS?

 **TIM** If wine is put in a decanter or a jug at home, oxygen reopens up all the different flavour elements within it. I will often pour my wines into a decanter at home just to see how it changes.

 **MIKEY** I've found most wines will benefit from a splash in the decanter, but you can't shine a turd. There are limitations.

 **MICHAEL** Aeration works for both aged and young wines. Aerating an aged wine opens the wine up and releases the beautiful bottle-aged aromatics and flavours. Young reds especially can have harder tannins. By aerating them, you can make these harder tannins softer and more palatable.

It's good to try new things. You know what's also good? Trying new things without pants on. When you buy wine online, you can be introduced to new plonk without leaving your snugly bugly bed. Blissssss.

But remember, it's important to taste new varieties. Try not to stick to what you know.

MIKEY There are over 1300 grape varieties used to make wine. Why stick to Shiraz and Sauvy? It'd be like listening to your favourite song over and over and over again to the exclusion of everything else. There is so much to explore. Get out there and dive in!

Sure, buying online means you lose the benefits a face-to-face recommendation can provide, but it's a *really* easy way to buy in larger quantities. Online outfits worth checking out are:

- Different Drop
- Wine Republic
- The Wine Society
- Organic-loving DRNKS.com.

There are also online retailers that offer monthly subscription services or curated cases like:

- The Wine Gallery
- Vinomofo
- Magnum & Queens Wine.

CHOOSE
YOUR
OWN
WINE-
VENTURE

51

**TRUE OR FALSE** **Large, commercial wineries are no good?**

 **MIKEY** It depends on the winery. Penfolds make amazing wines, as do the uber hipster producers keeping it real, going full rogue. Good wine is good wine and there are so many ways to measure this. I prefer wines with a story that communicates the philosophy of the producer as well as place. You're more likely to find these stories in smaller boutique wineries.

 **SAM** I think the big difference is that for any small producer you don't have the luxury of being able to blend away your mistakes or only select the very best barrels from a particular batch and grade the rest to a lower product. If you're a small producer you can't make wine 'disappear', you've got to face up to your mistakes and try to make the best of it. It's more of a heart-on-your-sleeve winemaking proposition, I suppose. While if you're a winemaker in a big company, you can downgrade wines.

Commercial producers do an amazingly consistent job, especially from a wine-quality perspective. But in terms of explaining to a consumer what the difference is, what they're going to get in the bottle, it's a lot more hard work to maintain quality when you're a small producer rather than a large one.

CHOOSE
YOUR
OWN
WINE-
VENTURE

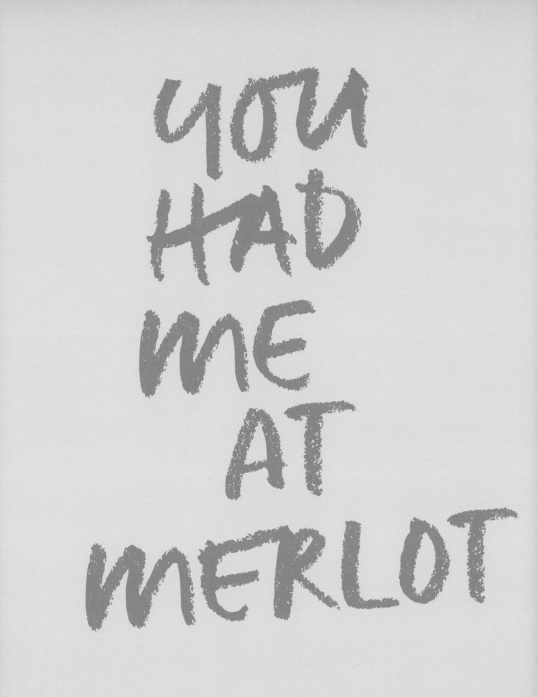

'THAT'S WHAT MINIMAL INTERVENTION IS ABOUT TO ME — LETTING THE FRUIT EXPRESS ITSELF… IT'S NOT [ABOUT] EXPRESSING THE IMPRINT OF THE WINEMAKER.'

Samantha Connew

BACK IN THE DAY, the French and Italians ruled Wine World like it was Westeros. Wines were named according to the area they were from, rather than the grapes they were jam-packed with. But in the last couple of decades, the rest of the world has risen up and said, 'Yeah, nah. We want to make it clearer to consumers what's in here, bud!' So now the practice of varietal labeling has become a thing. Mostly a New World thing, but a thing nonetheless. (I would list which countries use regional labeling over varietal for you, but we'll chat more about this later and I don't want to blow my word count listing most of Europe.)

'Wait, what?' you say. Okay, imagine you're looking for a French Pinot Noir; you wouldn't necessarily find one by scanning for 'French' or 'Pinot Noir' on the label. Instead you would keep an eye out for 'Burgundy', the appellation it's associated with. Or say you were jonesing to try an Italian Barbera, Dolcetto or Nebbiolo — you'd be on the lookout for the northwestern region of 'Piedmont'.

If this sounds a bit too intimidating and you're open to New World regions, scan away for labels bearing 'Pinot Noir' or 'Merlot' or whatever varietal you're looking for. Or better yet, ask a wine professional for help.

The more you drink and ask questions, the more you'll figure out which regions are known for which varieties. (Now THIS is a challenge I can get behind.) The thing is, though, there are currently over 1300 commercially available grape varieties. I could overwhelm you with an alphabetical list of grapes, including floral descriptions next to each, but we're here for a good time, not a long time, Brenda.

Instead, let's get to know some of the most common and iconic

YOU
HAD
ME
AT
MERLOT

varieties out there. That way, you can decide which wines you might like to get to know a little better. And what better way to do that than to humanise them? Which wine is a Susan? Which is a Pierre? Would your vino like rugby or reading? Would your plonk work in HR, or be an entrepreneur?

So here are twenty of Australia and New Zealand's grape varieties (and a handful of wine styles) anthropomorphised into people you could be friends with. (I've also thrown in a few of my personal faves for funsies.) Now, when you're trying to remember what Malbec tastes like you'll think bright, magenta-loving Prince instead of drawing a complete blank.

# GUESS WHO? (THE WINE EDITION)

The best way to start a (initially playful then increasingly emotionally violent) party game with your friends is to decide who is what varietal.

**Step One:** Decide which friend is in the hot seat.

**Step Two:** Proceed to list their most pronounced personality traits.

**Step Three:** Narrow this list down to three characteristics.

**Step Four:** Match these qualities to a grape varietal, comparing adjectives.

**Step Five:** Share your working with the rest of the class.

**Example:** You could describe me as fiery, resilient and an acquired taste, making me an excellent Gamay (a French varietal famous in Beaujolais, known for being zippy, high in acidity and selectively popular).

**N.B.** I will not be held responsible for any hurt feelings that may arise from this innocent party game.

# WINE-DERFUL WHITE WINE GRAPES

Before we dive in, let's get to know white wines as a whole. Let's go on a date. First up, know that white wine can be made from white OR red grapes. To make white wine, the juice is fermented without the grape skins and at a cooler temperature than red wine. Essentially the rule is, no skins = little to no colour[1]. The cooler conditions ensure that all those fresh and fruity flavours stay put. The wine then either goes into steel vats or oak barrels to be aged for a time. Oaked whites can then also undergo malolactic fermentation[2], giving the vino a slightly oily and creamy texture.

YOU HAD ME AT MERLOT

59

From there, the wine is (usually) filtered before bottling. Without filtering, the wine would be cloudy (which isn't necessarily a bad thing). Sulphites[3] are then added to preserve the vino. When it

---

[1] No hat, no play. No skins, no colour.

[2] **MALOLACTIC FERMENTATION** = a winemaking process (involving Oenoccocus Oeni bacteria) where tart malic acid gets converted into creamy lactic acid, resulting in a more velvety texture.

[3] **SULPHITES** = a widely used preservative in winemaking that helps prevent oxidation. We'll discuss sulphites further on pages 101–4 when talking about minimal intervention wines.

arrives at your table, your white wine will likely be served in a small, slim glass. The U-shaped bowl helps maintain aroma whilst keeping the wine cool.

Okay, now that you've been formally introduced, let's informally get to know the many personalities of white wine.

## CHARDONNAY

- Ranges from elegant, in cool climates, to more bold and fruity in warm climates
- Originally from Burgundy
- Often hastily written off for brassiness, but well deserving of a second chance

When I think of Chardonnay, I think of *RuPaul's Drag Race*. (If you don't know it, it's like *America's Next Top Model* for drag queens, but better.) That's because Chardy is a hardy varietal that has RANGE. Much like my all-time favourite contestant, Katya, Chardonnay can be dry and demure OR a complete party monster. Okay, not literally, but you get my point: Chardonnay has something for everyone.

This popular Burgundy native is always open to experimentation – a little barrel fermentation[4] here, some extended lees contact[5] there. She's particularly extra when she's grown in warmer climates, like South Australia and California: all that early-ripening heat pumps

---

[4] **BARREL FERMENTATION** = wine fermented in barrels rather than stainless steel. Often gives a more oaky quality, and also affects the wine's texture and structure.

[5] **LEES** = dead yeast that can add a creamy texture to the palate.
**EXTENDED LEES CONTACT** = the longer the contact with the must, the more pronounced the effect. Can range anywhere from months to years.

Chardonnay up with alcohol, making her brassy[6] AF. That's why some people tend to prefer her after a stint in a cooler, calming environment like France or New Zealand. She tends to have a bit more structure in her life and a bit less alcohol in her system when she's out of the heat – but she's also half the fun.

You can find flexxy Chardonnay all around the world, and in nearly all of Australia's 63 wine regions. If you're looking for her at her most big, bold and buttery, try something from the Riverina or Hunter Valley, NSW. But for the lady at her most elegant, have a bottle from Victoria's Yarra Valley, Adelaide Hills, Mornington Peninsula or WA's Margaret River.

**Fave meal:** You kidding me? Bish doesn't eat.

**Fave outfit:** Bodacious blonde wig. Sequined cape with matching catsuit. An oversized black fan.

**Fave song:** 'Young Hearts Run Free' by Candi Staton.

YOU HAD ME AT MERLOT

61

---

[6] **BRASSY** = harsh and a bit loud.

## On Aussie Chardonnay

**BEN**  I know that I've liked Chardonnays in the past, but I can't trust that they will be inherently great because I know that some Chardonnays taste like a stranger has urinated in my mouth.

**AMANDA**  Australia used to have a reputation for really big, ballsy, oaky Chardonnay, which we deserved. We now have more moderate Chardonnays. At one stage we actually went a bit too lean, but now we have a sense of moderation – medium-bodied, a combination of new and old oak, with that ingress[7] of oxygen that adds a little bit of texture to the wine.

## CHENIN BLANC

- Versatile, can do everything from dry to sweet to sparkling
- Originally from Loire Valley, France, but now ultra-famous in South Africa
- Often blended with other varieties

Chenin Blanc is a likeable little pocket rocket who is the *perfect* plus one. She's the kind of versatile legend who can oscillate between being very dry with your mates, extremely sweet to your gramps, and perfectly sparkling on a dance floor. Maybe it's because she's been based all around the world — everywhere from South Africa,

[7]  **INGRESS** = a little sneaky, sneaky addition of something.

Argentina, California and France's Loire Valley. But Stellenbosch, South Africa, is where she's most comfy (and most widely cultivated). She's known as Steen around there.

Down our end of the world, Chenin Blanc is mostly seen as a blending variety, but you can find her holding her own in WA (particularly in the Swan District and Margaret River, where she's super voluptuous and fruity). And guess what? If you like her, you may also like her svelte bestie, Verdelho . New friends ahoy!

**Fave meal:** She may not be American, but her festive spirit means she LOVES herself some Thanksgiving turkey with cranberry sauce.

**Fave outfit:** A pale yellow, 50s-style dress with a tropical pattern. Chenin Blanc froths over the way it spins when she dances.

**Fave song:** 'Happy' by Pharrell.

you HAD me AT mERLOT

## GEWÜRZTRAMINER

- Aromatic white wine that's great with spicy cuisine
- Low in acidity, high in alcohol
- Homeland is the foothills of the Alps, grows well in cooler climates

This aromatic wine has been described as the adult version of Moscato. He's the boy-next-door who grew up and read *The Game*.

Without a doubt, he's a charmer. But he's actually not that sweet. Gewürztraminer is the guy who negs you by telling you how gorgeous your dress would be on that attractive waitress.

Despite not being in high demand, he's the kind who treats dating like his own un-filmed version of *The Bachelor*. But Gewürztraminer can still somehow win you over. Maybe it's his extremely floral cologne? Or the hint of lychee hiding in his kiss. Whatever it is, this full-bodied professional flirt is low in acidity and high in alcohol, meaning he can be a LOT of fun. (I admit to loving him throughout my 20s, despite myself.)

Gewürztraminer bases himself mainly in France's Alsace and Italy's Alto Adige regions, but is also known for his increasing presence in Australia's very own Clare and Eden Valleys, as well as NZ's Marlborough region. Ask for him at a boutique wine retailer if you want to have a tempestuous (and potentially unhealthy) love affair.

**Fave meal:** A fragrant fish curry, packed with ginger. He's an adventurer at heart, so the more exotic the better.

**Fave outfit:** The sad cap, tracky dacks and busted tee ensemble that Shia LaBeouf was rocking/not rocking in 2016.

**Fave song:** 'The Hills' by The Weeknd.

## GRÜNER VELTLINER

- Light, zesty white; a more intrepid version of Sauvignon Blanc
- High in acidity
- Grows almost exclusively in Austria

Grüner Veltliner is a neat freak who grew up in eastern Austria and is considered their beloved golden boy. Primarily based in Austria, Czech Republic and Slovakia, he's recently made his way to South Australia's Adelaide Hills region and the Canberra District, as well as NZ's Gisborne, Marlborough, Waipara and Central Otago regions.

This old soul, with a thing for crisp freshness and minerality, is a foodie through and through – a young Matt Preston (cravat and all). If there's a rich dish to eat, this hungry gent will get himself near it ASAP. He's a dry and zesty character with high acidity and some spicy views. So if you're dining with him, probz don't bring up the moon landing or who killed JFK over your cheese platter.

*Fave meal:* A traditional Austrian Wiener Schnitzel (mostly because it's fun to say).

*Fave outfit:* A crisp navy suit and cravat for the win.

*Fave song:* The *MasterChef* theme song.

YOU HAD ME AT MERLOT

65

## PINOT GRIS/GRIGIO

- Grey-ish grape that's a mutation of Pinot Noir
- Gris = French-style. Silky, full-bodied white
- Grigio = Italian-style. Light, crisp white

Pinot Gris/Grigio is like the Pink Lady from 'Grease' who people half-remember[8]. The one with that shady marine pen pal who's been deployed to Korea. You know, the one who wears a kerchief around her neck. You know, who thinks Jan's pairing of Twinkies with wine is basic. MARTY! Martina Maraschino for the win.

This grape is a clever little mutation of Pinot Noir whose pink skin doesn't have quite enough colour to make red wine. Hence the 'pinot' nod. Meanwhile the 'gris/grigio' refers to its 'grey' colour – gris in French, grigio in Italian. This descriptor is a slight misnomer though, seeing how when winemakers leave the grape juice in contact with its skins, a pale pink (not sad grey) wine results. Much like Marty, Pinot G is heavily perfumed, and it's a similar weight to Pinot Noir (more on old mate Peeny later). Flavour and acidity-wise, there's not a heck of a lot going on.

### TRUE OR FALSE   Pinot Grigio and Gris are the same?

Same grape, different styles. Whether it's produced in France, Oz, NZ or beyond – you can expect the Italian-style Pinot Grigio (which is picked earlier) to be lighter and brighter with more pronounced

[8]   To be fair, maybe I just half-remember Marty. Frenchy and Rizzo were always my favourites.

citrus flavours. Meanwhile, johnny-come-lately Pinot Gris is produced in the Alsace style as a throwback to its French roots. It tends to be richer, more full-bodied and packed with more spices than Grigio. So yeah, same varietal, but different vibes. Much like Shiraz versus Syrah.

Try a Gris from Alsace or a Grigio from Friuli in northeast Italy for the OG examples of what this lady can do. In Australia, she's been around since the 80s and you'll find her at her most energetic in cool-climate areas like Vic's Mornington Peninsula, King Valley and Grampians; NSW's Orange and Mudgee; SA's Adelaide Hills; and Tassie.

In NZ, you'll find super fresh Pinot Gris in maritime climates like Marlborough, Hawke's Bay and Gisborne. Get to know her. She'll have you singing a wop ba-ba lu-bop a wop bam boom.

**Fave meal:** Roast pork with homemade apple sauce. (No carbs. She's watching her figure for the dance.)

**Fave outfit:** White nightie and a red kimono (á la the sleepover scene).

**Fave music:** 'La Bamba' by Los Lobos & Gipsy Kings.

## RIESLING
- Complex white wine with a great ability to age
- Originally from Germany
- Grows well in SA's Clare and Eden Valleys

YOU HAD ME AT MERLOT

67

Riesling is the suffering intellectual of the white wine world. He's the kind of guy who would insist you pronounce his name 'Reeceling', not 'Reezeling', then pretend it's not a big deal. He's a frustrated German poet at heart, a moody dreamer who doesn't adapt to different social situations all that seamlessly. Oh, but he's still a critic's delight. Did you see that thing he did in Alsace? That performance in Austria? Or his cameo in Australia's very own Eden and Clare Valleys? So complex. So unexpected. A little sweet, even.

Riesling ages well because of his high acidity. He's the kind of dude who gets better looking as he gets older. And even though he's not as well known as his peers Sauvignon Blanc and Chardonnay, he's a unique character who has a lot to say.

> **Fave meal:** Gluten-free chicken and vegetable pie (or something equally low FODMAP).
>
> **Fave outfit:** Mustard-yellow tweed suit, dark floral cologne, brown brogues and tortoise-shell glasses. Glasses may or may not have real lenses in them.
>
> **Fave song:** Piano Concerto op. 42 by Arnold Schoenberg.

# AN ODE TO RIESLING

**SAM** I think people have this conception that Riesling doesn't display the complexity of a great Chardonnay. But there are many ways to impact a Riesling from a grape-growing and a winemaking point of view, for example, whether to employ skin contact, what vessel you should ferment it in, how long to leave the wine on lees post-ferment, etc.

I certainly think Rieslings are some of the most exciting wines coming out of Australia now because they're starting to demonstrate where they come from. It's not just Clare Valley Riesling and Eden Valley Riesling anymore. There are great wines from other regions – Tasmania, Great Southern in WA. They speak of their regions so transparently, with more unique terroir[9] characteristics than possibly any other white grape variety, apart from Semillon.

To me, Riesling has certainly laid claim to being a top white varietal – the power, the complexity with age as well. It's shown an ability to age because the pH is so low. That's the big factor in the age-ability of Riesling. The low pH acts as a natural preservative for the wine. So get one from a good producer in a good region and you're home and hosed.

*YOU HAD ME AT MERLOT*

## SAUVIGNON BLANC
- Originally from Loire Valley, now a New Zealand icon
- Refreshing, savoury white that varies according to region and whether it's fermented in stainless steel or oak. Predominantly un-oaked
- Light-medium body, moderately high in acidity

[9] **TERROIR** = a French term referring to the environment in which a wine is produced, everything from the climate and soil to the surrounding flora and fauna.

Sauvignon Blanc reminds me of Tilda Swinton playing an ice queen á la *Chronicles of Narnia*. Or better yet, as a terrifying set of amoral CEO twins in Bong Joon-ho's film *Okja*. This may make Sauvy sound like a bloodthirsty, corporate-friendly psychopath. But the fact is, Sauvy really is sharp, to the point and sometimes as biting as a lemon.

There's power packed into this increasingly popular grape. That's why it's become such a mainstay for regions like Oz's Adelaide Hills (SA), Margaret River (WA), King and Goulburn Valleys (Vic), Tasmania, Orange (NSW), New Zealand's Marlborough and Hawke's Bay, as well as France's Loire Valley (particularly Sancerre and Pouilly-Fumé). Let the record show that Aussies' most beloved Sauvy comes from NZ[10].

While the typical Kiwi Sauvy smells all things green (think grass, green leaves and even asparagus), French Sauvy tends to have a more mineral bent (think stones and wet chalk). Sauvy tends to be super dry and high in acidity. French Sauvy especially. However, if those grapes get overripe, they can lose their characteristic smell. That's why they flourish in cool climates, away from the equator. Much like Tilda Swinton.

**Fave meal:** Ceviche with a crisp green salad. And an extra side of greens.

**Fave outfit:** All-white pantsuit. Vintage fur stole. Kind of like The Duchess from *My Dad Wrote A Porno*.

**Fave song:** Anything steely and electronic. Think 'Baptism' by Crystal Castles.

[10] We import that Kiwi gold like we're bunkering down for the apocalypse.

## SEMILLON

- Full-bodied, popular white. Blends well with Sauvignon Blanc and Muscadelle
- Originally from Bordeaux, now big in the Hunter Valley
- Often used to make dessert wines

Semillon is the matriarch of a successful farming dynasty. She has seen it all, done it all and aged surprisingly well. (Must use a banger moisturiser or some of that SK-II shizz that Cate Blanchett likes so much.)

Her natural resilience (and penchant for flannelette) means she's not that fashion-forward, but she gets the job done right. Semillon is easy to work with and always gets high yields.

If you want to try some of her dessert wines or get to know her at her most herbaceous, drop in to NSW's Riverina or in the warm and humid Hunter Valley. Or if you're looking for something more weighty and structured, say 'G'day!' to her in SA's Barossa and Clare Valleys or WA's Margaret River.

YOU HAD ME AT MERLOT

71

Fave meal: A simple picnic of fresh farm produce.

Fave outfit: Aforementioned flannel shirt paired with a Tweety Bird tee from the late '90s, mum jeans and R.M. Williams.

Fave song: 'Around Here' by Thelma Plum.

## VIOGNIER

- Textured, full-bodied white with similar qualities to Chardonnay
- Low in acidity, high in alcohol
- Originally from southern France

Viognier is the new guy on the block in Australia, but he's been around southern France for years. He's that nice bloke with a Jon Hamm-style Dad bod (though he can be a bit grumpy when faced with the heat). He's textured and full-bodied like his mate Chardonnay, but with a softer, gentler character. He can be a bit unpredictable, though, and his low yields means he doesn't give much away. This means he isn't necessarily the most economical horse for winemakers to put a punt on.

But who can resist an approachable foodie who often smells like tangerines and mango? Or even vanilla and nutmeg, when he's been hanging around oak? He even manages to maintain his dry humour with surprisingly high alcohol content, low acidity and a slightly oily sensation on the mid-palate. What a man, what a man, what a mighty good man.

Visit him in Canberra or South Australia (particularly Eden Valley, Langhorne Creek, McLaren Vale and Adelaide Hills). Or if you're feeling like you want to head off the beaten track, find him in the river region of southeast Australia – the Riverina, Murray Valley and Riverland. In NZ, he hangs about Waiheke Island and Hawke's Bay. He's worth the hike.

**Fave meal:** Something hearty but spicy, like teriyaki tofu.

**Fave outfit:** Polo shirt, shorts and sensible trainers.
(Effectively, a Dad outfit.)

**Fave song:** 'Whatta Man' by Salt 'N' Pepa (featuring En Vogue).


## VERDELHO
- Originally from Madeira, Portugal
- Tropical, fruity white with high acidity
- Grows especially well in Margaret River and Hunter Valley


Verdelho is like one of those aspirational Insta models who hetero men and queer women fall over themselves for. She is just in another league from the rest of us plebs. But while Verdelho is intense and stunning, she can be highly acidic, and this early-ripening, tropical siren is very sensitive in nature. Verdelho is susceptible to phylloxera[11] and high sugar content. So if you're more than ten minutes late to your dinner date, know that you are dead to her. DEAD.

Originally from the island of Madeira, Portugal, Verdelho has got a taste for lime and honeysuckle and is beloved in Argentina, Spain and Australia. And she's not just a pretty face. Lady has travelled and knows her history. She once visited the last emperor of Russia, Tsar Nicolas II, on a state visit (true story).

To find her at her most tropical in Oz, you'll have to make a pilgrimage to WA's Margaret River and Swan District, or NSW's

you HAD ME AT MERLOT

73

[11] **PHYLLOXERA** = a tiny aphid that munches on grape roots. There was a huge scourge across Europe in the late 1800s.

Riverina. Head to the Hunter Valley to find her at her most balanced. Alternatively, SA's Langhorne Creek will give you the opportunity to see her transform into a fortified version of herself.

> **Fave meal:** She loves Vietnamese. Prawn-and-cucumber rice paper rolls would be a safe bet.
>
> **Fave outfit:** Backless gown made of jade-green silk. Alexander Wang heels. (Do not be shocked if girl has gone commando.)
>
> **Fave song:** 'Why Don't You Do Right' by Jessica Rabbit.

## Super happy fun task for winos

Ooh, so many delicious white wines to taste! List the top three whites you're keen to try next.

*1.* _____

_____

*2.* _____

_____

*3.* _____

_____

# WINE-DERFUL RED WINE GRAPES

Time to get to know red a bit better! Unlike white wine, red vino has GOTS to come from red or black grapes as the grape skins give the wine its rich, full colour. So after these beauties are grown, harvested, de-stemmed and crushed, they are put in an environment where yeast can thrive and fermentation can begin. That's where the grapes' natural sugar gets converted into alcohol. The longer the red wine is fermented, the more sugar is consumed. If most or all of the sugar is consumed, you've got yourself a dry red.

Red wines are then aged in oak, concrete, amphora or steel for months to years, depending on the winemaker. This is (usually) followed by a process of fining[12] and/or filtration[13] to polish off the wine and get it ready for bottling.

By the time it gets to you, your red will either be served in a big Burgundy glass[14] or a taller Bordeaux-style glass.[15] The balloon-like Burgundy glasses are ideal for aromatic reds like Pinot Noir, while the slimmer Bordeaux glasses are more versatile and suit most other reds.

Now that initial introductions have been made, let's dig a little deeper.

*you HAD me AT mERLOT*

[12] **FINING** = adding a protein or additive to remove astringency and clarify the wine.

[13] **FILTRATION** = the process of filtering the wine to be more polished and maintain microbial stability within the bottle.

[14] **BURGUNDY GLASS** = rounder, bowl-like wine glasses that better capture the wine's aromas. Perfect for more delicate vinos like Pinot Noir.

[15] **BORDEAUX GLASS** = taller, less bowl-like wine glasses that encourage wine to head to the back of the mouth. Ideal for full-bodied reds.

## CABERNET FRANC

- Medium-bodied savoury red with medium acidity
- Originally from western France
- Popular blending grape, particularly with Cabernet Sauvignon and Merlot

Cabernet Franc is the Idris Elba of the wine world – rich, attractive and a little bit cheeky. With a charming, yet subtly herbaceous fragrance, Cabernet Franc is lighter and spicier than his well-known relative Cabernet Sauvignon.

Originally from the Basque country of western France, Cabernet Franc is the medium-bodied, medium-acidity type who would love to go to dinner with you. His kiss has this savoury quality that might pleasantly surprise you: think roast capsicum in a glass.

**FAST FACT:**

Cabernet Sauvignon is the result of breeding Cabernet Franc and Sauvignon Blanc.

He's mostly based in France, Italy, Chile and the US, but in Australia you can find him in WA's Margaret River and Great Southern regions. In NZ, he resides in Hawke's Bay and Auckland. But be aware, he's not always the single-varietal kind of grape. He loves to hang with Cabernet Sauvignon and Merlot and can be found most famously in the iconic Bordeaux Blend.

**Fave meal:** Braised Portobello mushrooms with angel hair pasta and fresh thyme. That he made. Just for you.

**Fave outfit:** A tuxedo worthy of James Bond.

**Fave song:** 'Skyfall' by Adele.

## CABERNET SAUVIGNON

- Full-bodied red with dark fruit flavours
- Originally from Bordeaux
- Blends well with Merlot and Cabernet Franc

How to describe Cabernet Sauvignon? Think Oprah. This small, thick-skinned power player will age well. She's iconic, full-bodied and popular. Young Cabernet Sauvignon packs a punch with loads of tannins, colour and medium acidity. Dark berry flavours are her trademark, but she's also open to blending with Merlot and Cabernet Franc. So YOU get a great wine, YOU get a great wine. EVERYBODY gets a great wine!

Guarded at heart, it often takes a while for this lady to warm to you. But when she's in her element – HELLOOOO – she is the best. She thrives in mild maritime climates with well-draining soil like Bordeaux, France; Napa Valley, California; Chile; as well as Coonawarra (SA) and Margaret River (WA), Australia. However, she's a traveller at heart, so you'll find her roaming the globe anywhere there's a chance for her to flourish (and have an 'Aha!' moment).

you HAD me AT mERLOT

Fave meal: Her latest mac and cheese recipe. Available now in *O Magazine*.

Fave outfit: The iconic scarlet Vera Wang gown she rocked at the Legends Ball.

Fave song: Anything by her fave singer, Snatam Kaur.

## GAMAY

- Higher in acidity and lower in tannin than Pinot Noir
- Bright and fruity red
- The Beaujolais region's golden girl (though it can also be found in Loire Valley, Cali's Napa Valley and around Oz's cooler regions)

This fiery redhead punk is the reason the French region of Beaujolais is suh hot right now. She's the acerbic older sister of thin-skinned Pinot Noir[16]. This is the kind of woman who can rock an edgy bob and verbally ruin you if you make fun of her baby brother. Maybe it's because this rabble-rouser matures a lot quicker than her little sibling. (Or maybe she's just got anger management issues. Evidence points both ways.)

With a dry sense of humour, Gamay is higher in acidity and lower in tannin than Pinot Noir. She's a lot brighter than Pinot Noir, giving her more punchy fruitiness and a juicy quality.

In Oz, she hangs around Victoria in Gippsland, Rutherglen, Red Hill, Beechworth and Yarra Valley. In NZ, you can find her lurking in very sneaky corners of Hawke's Bay[17].

Fave meal: She's a socialist, so she loves to share a nice charcuterie board. (And who doesn't love bite-sized snacks?)

Fave outfit: Her boyfriend's biker jacket and an old black slip. Combat boots. Rings on every finger. Piercings loaded up on both ears and through her septum.

Fave song: 'None of your business, you fascist pig.' (Alright, mate. Chill out.)

[16] Flick to page 83 for more info on Pinot Noir.
[17] There are only about eight hectares of Gamay in NZ so far.

## GARNACHA/GRENACHE

- Medium-bodied, high in alcohol, light in colour
- Most iconic in northern Spain and Southern Rhône
- Blends well with Syrah and Mataro to create GSM

79

Garnacha (or Grenache to his Parisian friends) is the forgotten middle child of his big Spanish family. This cheeky trickster is not as well regarded as his stately older brother Tempranillo, but they still love to hang out. Garnacha is known for lightening the mood with his ripe and spicy character, and spreading juicy gossip at dull parties. Maybe this is why this strawberry-blonde shit-stirrer is taken less seriously in Spain. It's possibly why he's often seen gallivanting in France, Italy, China and Australia.

If you want to hook up with him in Oz, you'll have to hitch a ride to the McLaren Vale and Barossa[18] regions of South Australia, where he's known for doing his own thing and producing great rosé[19]. He's also known to mix with Shiraz (Syrah) and Mourvèdre (Mataro), creating those delish GSM blends that South Australia is famous for.

> **Fave meal:** A herb-heavy, three-hat meal that he will DEFINITELY reimburse you for next week. Promise.
>
> **Fave outfit:** His bro's hand-me-downs and a well-textured quiff.
>
> **Fave song:** 'Return of The Mack' by Mark Morrison, on repeat, as he cruises around town in his dad's beat-up Beamer.

## MALBEC

- Full-bodied red with deep purple colouring
- Originally from Cahors region in southwest France, but iconic in Argentina
- Medium acidity, medium tannin

Malbec and Prince have a lot in common. They're both big personalities with a love of magenta. You can spot Malbec from his deep purple-red colouring.

---

[18] Barossa Valley has some of the oldest Grenache vineyards in the world, dating back to 1850.

[19] More about the process for making rosé can be found on pp 104–8.

Malbec may come from the Cahors region in southwest France, but he's famous for living in Argentina. He's mostly planted there and loves the hot days and cold nights at high elevation. This is the secret behind his kick of acidity, the flamboyant personality we so love.

Malbec is a character in his own right, but also blends well. When he spends time in chillier France, he's known for being meaty and peppery, while in Argentina, he's lower in acidity and extra fruity. Think raspberry and plum (and maybe even a sniff of tobacco, if he's been hanging around oak).

If you want to get to know him in Australia, head to moderate climates like WA's Margaret River and Great Southern, as well as SA's Clare Valley and Langhorne Creek.

**Fave meal:** Anything with big, funky flavours. Blue cheese? Yes, please.

**Fave outfit:** Sparkling purple coat with chainmail detail, white ruffled shirt and high-waisted black trousers with military buttons, black leather shoes shined to perfection. Amen.

**Fave song:** 'Purple Rain' by Prince and The Revolution.

YOU
HAD
ME
AT
MERLOT

81

## MERLOT

- Originally from Bordeaux
- Medium to full-bodied red with a rep for being middle of the road. Underdog of the wine world
- Known for its red fruit flavours and smooth finish

Merlot is that approachable but slightly earnest gal who comes from a big family in the southwest of France. Unlike Cabernet Franc and Cabernet Sauvignon, Merlot is rounder and softly spoken – a medium to full-bodied accountant who has a rep for being a bit boring. If she wasn't called 'Merlot', she'd probably be a Susan.

But when cultivated appropriately in cool to warm climates, she's a plummy mixer who puts flesh on the bones of any good convo. Maybe that's why she gets along so well with Cabernet Sauvignon, who manages to fill the gaps in Merlot's often tangent-packed stories. Home for this serious lady is Bordeaux's St Emilion and Pomerol. However, she's also lived in Italy, the US (particularly California and Washington) and Chile. She's made her presence known in most of Oz, bar the coolest climates, showing some great fruity work in SA's Barossa Valley and McLaren Vale. To meet her when she's hanging with Cabernet (and a little more structured), visit places with well-draining soil like WA's Margaret River and SA's Coonawarra. In NZ, she does well in regions like Hawke's Bay, Northland and Auckland.

Fave meal: Grilled lamb chops. No sides.

Fave outfit: A well-tailored grey pant suit.

Fave song: '5, 6, 7, 8' by Steps.

## PINOT NOIR

- Almost translucent red with silky tannins
- Notoriously difficult to grow
- Originally from Burgundy

There are two people who should come to mind when you think of Pinot Noir – Paul Giamatti as that sad bloke from *Sideways* and Tituss Burgess singing in *Unbreakable Kimmy Schmidt*. (If you don't know what I'm talking about, put down this book on the immediate and YouTube 'unbreakable kimmy schmidt peeno noir'.) Let's instead think of someone who's beautiful, but finicky. Let's imagine a charismatic, but anally retentive aviator and film director[20].

Originally from Burgundy, France, Pinot is an unpredictable number who can be oh so elegant, but easy to spoil, no thanks to his sensitive nature. This is because our delicate friend Pinot is super thin-skinned (literally) and susceptible to illness (every disease, mould, fungus and pest known to vines). But when he's good – OH, HONEY – he's good. He may be paler and lighter than ballsy Cabernet and less tannic, but he has great length.

You can find this gorgeously aromatic mister in cool climates such as France's Burgundy, Champagne and Alsace regions; Germany; USA's Oregon; and New Zealand. In NZ, he particularly flourishes in Martinborough, Marlborough and Central Otago. Lately he's been doing just fine in cooler parts of Australia (like Gippsland, Yarra Valley[21],

*you HAD me AT merlot*

83

[20]  Imagine Howard Hughes. (Shout out to the guy I met on Bumble who gave me this idea!)

[21]  I'm very into Mac Forbes in Yarra Valley.

Mornington Peninsula, Geelong, Macedon Ranges and most of central Victoria TBH, and even Tasmania[22]).

> **Fave meal:** Seventy-three peas of the exact same size and shape.
>
> **Fave outfit:** Leonardo DiCaprio's early get-up in *The Aviator*.
>
> **Fave song:** 'Peeno Noir' by Tituss Burgess.

## SANGIOVESE

- Adaptable grape with mutations across Italy
- Savoury red with flavours ranging from earthy to fruity
- High in acidity, high in tannin

Sangiovese is the hot itinerant farmhand of the wine world. You know the type – dark curly hair, shirt sticking to his sweaty, sun-kissed chest, bronzed biceps that can make you lose track of . . . lose track of . . .

Sorry, what?

Sangiovese! Sangiovese. Hi.

From central Italy, this shirtless wonder is adaptable to most environments, with flavours varying from very fruit-forward to earthy. When he's carefully cultivated and given some boundaries, rustic Sangiovese can show you the best of Tuscany. Try the Chianti Classico from the cooler hills of central Tuscany or Brunello di

[22] Tolpuddle Vineyard and Chatto Wines do a mean Pinot Noir in Tassie.

Montalcino from the warmer south (if you're feeling fancy).
If you're looking for him in Oz – which can be tricky as he doesn't
tend to travel outside of Italy – search him out in Mediterranean
climates like South Australia. McLaren Vale and Barossa Valley
are your safest bet. Heathcote in Victoria is also worth a look.
In NZ, he's at his most developed in warmer regions like Auckland
and Hawke's Bay. The perfect varietal to take a tumble in the
hay with.

> **Fave meal:** A long lunch starring his homemade pasta
> with Puttanesca sauce.
>
> **Fave outfit:** His birthday suit.
>
> **Fave song:** The sound of your racing heart.

you HAD me AT mERLOT

## SHIRAZ/SYRAH

- Same grape, different feels
- Syrah tends to be lighter and more delicate
- Shiraz is often bolder and full-bodied

Shiraz/Syrah is an increasingly popular grape with very
different offerings. This varietal epitomises the nature/nurture
argument. It's like a female/male set of twins who grew up in
different families. While the gal loves rock climbing and *Street
Fighter*, the guy likes Rimbaud and sketching rude nudes.
Let's just say, they had VERY different upbringings.

Let's break it down. Shiraz is the Aussie name for Syrah, a grape native to the northern Rhône valley in France. Shiraz is now more widely planted in Australia than in northern Rhône, because this baller lady loves hot regions like the Barossa Valley, McLaren Vale, Clare Valley, Eden Valley, Heathcote and Hunter Valley. She's richly textured, dark and can be peppery (in the right mood).

Her brother's northern Rhône vibes are quite different – more delicate, with less alcohol in his system. When New World growers – Australia, South Africa or New Zealand (Hawke's Bay, Waiheke Island, Martinborough and the Wairarapa in particular) – want to emulate Syrah's more elegant style, they indicate this by calling the wine Syrah rather than Shiraz. (Plot twist: Americans tend to split the difference between the two styles, but still call it Syrah.) But don't be fooled, Shiraz is just as much, if not more fun than her twin. Different horses for different courses, you know?

**Fave meal:** She says tomayto, he says tomahto.

**Fave outfit:** She likes gumboots, he likes Gucci.

**Fave song:** 'Let's Call the Whole Thing Off' by Ella Fitzgerald and Louis Armstrong.

## TEMPRANILLO

- Iconic grape from Rioja
- Medium to full-bodied red with red fruit flavours and a smooth finish
- Low to medium acidity, soft tannins

Tempranillo is the Spanish diplomat of the wine world. He's a highly regarded, cigar-smoking icon who makes his mark in regions like Rioja and Ribera del Duero. He lives mostly in Spain and Portugal, but can also be found in South Africa, Australia (Heathcote, Orange, Canberra, McLaren Vale, Adelaide Hills and Barossa Valley), Argentina, and US states like California and Oregon.

He's the full-bodied, big brother of Garnacha (known to most as Grenache, thanks to his gap year in France). Low acid, soft tannins, minimal drama. As the favourite child, Tempranillo gets taken a lot more seriously and is respected for his hardiness in the face of Spain's low rainfall. Ripening earlier than other Spanish grapes[23], he has a relatively neutral flavour profile, so hangs with his fun younger brother Garnacha a lot. Big plum and strawberry flavours are his thing, as is being aged in oak. He's often referred to as Spain's 'noble grape' (which Garnacha claims is 'Totally fine, not even an issue').

**Fave meal:** Lasagna. Lasagna. Lasagna.

**Fave outfit:** A stately three-piece suit. Perfectly slicked-back hair.

**Fave song:** 'Money' by The Flying Lizards.

*you HAD me AT mERLOT*

87

[23]   Tempranillo's early ripening puts the *temprano* [early] in Tempranillo.

## Super happy fun task for winos

Who knew there were so many varieties of red?! List the top three
you'd like to now taste.

1. _____

_____

2. _____

_____

3. _____

_____

# STYLES, NOT GRAPES

These kids may not be common grape varieties per se, but I'll give
them arms and legs anyway because I'm lunch-drunk right now.

## FORTIFIED WINES

Fortified wines are the *Golden Girls* of the wine world – underrated,
not so trendy, but bloody fabulous. Most methods of making fortified
wines were created ~~in Miami, Florida in the late 80s~~ by Europeans on
the high seas throughout the 1700s. By adding a distilled spirit (usually
brandy) to wine during the fermentation process, yeast stops munching
through the sugar, leaving extra sweetness behind. The result?

A thicker, more alcoholic elixir with a longer shelf life. The perfect way to treat yourself, much like an ep (or eight) of *The Golden Girls*.

Meet the ladies for yourself.

## Sherry AKA Apera

- Wide range of styles from dry to sweet
- Originally from Andalucia, though does well in Rutherglen
- Referred to as 'Sherry' when from Jerez and 'Apera' outside of Spain

Ooh, honey, there's no better introduction to fortified wines than Sherry. She's like Dorothy – the tall, sardonic divorcee of the bunch. Her style ranges from light, dry Fino all the way to sticky sweet Pedro Ximénez, but I reckon she's at her best when she's as dry as a desert and as powerful as a woman spurned.

While Sherry loves a nice meal out, remember not to treat her like your average table wine. Otherwise you'll soon be on the floor wondering how this old white lady stole your dignity with such steely grace.

While this complex lady is native to Jerez in Andalucia, Spain (and should technically only be called Sherry if from there), she can be found trotting around the globe. In Oz and NZ, we've referred to her as 'Apera' since 2011. You'll find her in the Barossa and Rutherglen, as well as Auckland when you venture further afield. Tim recommends starting with biodynamic Pennyweight Winery in Beechworth, who do a few different styles of Apera.

YOU HAD ME AT MERLOT

**Fave meal:** At her driest, she loves a spread of salami, olives and cheese.

**Fave outfit:** Blush-pink pantsuit. Long string of pearls. Sensible shoes.

**Fave song:** *The Golden Girls* theme song.

## Vermouth

- Lightly fortified wine with infused botanicals
- Popular aperitif in Italy and France
- Can be consumed neat or with a splash of tonic water

Vermouth is the Sophia of fortified wines. A real Estelle Getty. Straight-talking and often spicy, unsweetened vermouth has bite, much like Dorothy's elderly mother has a striking lack of filter. (And I'm not so sure it's because of the stroke.)

While she's been a popular aperitif in Italy and France since the 18th century, this lightly fortified lady is gaining ground in Oz, too. If you're in Sydney, you can get to know her better at Banksii Vermouth Bar & Bistro. She can range anywhere from sweet to dry, white to red. At her best, you can enjoy her one-on-one or with a splash of tonic water. One thing's for sure: she'll always have a wine base with botanicals infused (and an outrageous story to boot).

**Fave meal:** Green olives and vodka.

**Fave outfit:** Yellow cardigan that's sturdy enough to survive both her nursing home burning down and a hurricane. Floral patterned dress. Signature oversized specs.

**Fave song:** *The Golden Girls* theme song.


## Port

- Originally from Portugal, referred to as 'Tawny' or 'Vintage' otherwise
- Most recognised as fortified dessert wine
- Comes in range of styles including ruby, white, tawny and rosé

Remember Blanche, the lover (not fighter) from *The Golden Girls*? Sweet, red fortified Port is just like her: a Southern belle with a flair for the dramatic. Port is not above stomping her feet. (Not even kidding. This is a style of wine stored in open vats and traditionally stomped on by feet every day.)

This confident lady is originally from Portugal and is a sweet, rich delight. I mean, she's rich enough that she owns the house all the gal pals are living in. Her style varies dramatically, her colours ranging from white to rosé, ruby and even tawny. Her tastes also vary widely: from blackberries to caramel to chocolate. She's a modern woman with broad tastes. And why the heck not?

YOU HAD ME AT MERLOT

Since real Port is only from Portugal, it helps to keep an eye out for words like 'Tawny' and 'Vintage'[24] on fortified wine labels if you want to meet her in Oz. She's especially ripe, robust and heavy in tannins in SA's Barossa (particularly Seppeltsfield), Victoria's Rutherglen, and NSW's Riverina.

**Fave meal:** Stinky blue cheese that's the yin to her yang.

**Fave outfit:** Turquoise silk dress with shoulder pads to the sky. Large gold clip-on earrings.

**Fave song:** *The Golden Girls* theme song.

## Tokay AKA Topaque

- Originally from Tokay-Hegyalija, northeastern Hungary
- Tokay from Hungary, 'Topaque' outside of Hungary
- A blend of wine and botrytis-affected grape juice

Oh, Tokay. Sweet, sweet Tokay. You are the Rose/Betty White of the fortified wines. Tokay may seem silly, but this lady has lived a life.

Much like absent-minded Rose, Tokay arose from a series of magical accidents. The story goes that Tokay was discovered by mistake in the 17th century when one harvest was picked late[25] out of fear of imminent attack from approaching Turkish armies. Tokay then went on to be the It girl in the royal courts of France, Prussia and Russia. If you're looking for her in

[24] Indicative of styles, rather than as an 'AKA for Port'.
[25] Being picked late resulted in botrytis-affected grape juice.

Oz, Rutherglen have made Tokay-style wine for nearly
100 years. (You'll have to call it Topaque though. Sorry 'bout it.)

**Fave meal:** She cuts through a rich, creamy cheese soufflé
like a boss.

**Fave outfit:** Light blue, collared blouse and matching skirt.
Giant pearl earrings.

**Fave song:** *The Golden Girls* theme song.

## MOSCATO

* Lightly sparkling wine that's low in alcohol and usually sweet
* Made from Muscat Blanc or Moscatel
* Originally from Piedmont

Usually made from Muscat Blanc or Moscatel, Moscato is a fun
nan who makes teenagers feel old. She's basically @baddiewinkle
– Internet legend/fashion icon/borrower of her great-
granddaughter's clothes/badass in her eighties who knows how
to rock a psychedelic crop top and short shorts. Moscato is sweet,
traditionally low in alcohol and a little bubbly, making her a solid
choice for family gatherings. That is, she won't get you drunk and
encourage you to talk politics with Uncle Greg.

Despite growing up in Piedmont, Italy, Moscato now grows
everywhere. She's known for sweet vibes of peach, nectarine and
orange blossom and has even had Drake's attention (see 'Fave

Song' below for deets). Much like Baddiewinkle owes Rihanna for Twitter followers, Moscato is indebted heavily to hip-hop for her popularity.

You can find her in NSW's Hunter Valley, Orange and Mudgee; northern Tasmania; SA's Adelaide Hills, Clare Valley and Langhorne Creek; Victoria's Geelong and King Valley; and Queensland's Granite Belt.

**Fave meal:** Red-hot spicy chicken wings. Anything with a bit of heat.

**Fave outfit:** Camouflage mesh tee with sunshine yellow overalls. White hi-tops and a bedazzled walking stick.

**Fave song:** 'Do It Now' by Drake.

## ORANGE WINE

- White wine that's had extended contact with grape skins and seeds
- Practice originated in Georgia
- Often uses fewer preservatives, favours wild over cultured yeasts

Orange (or 'Amber') wine is that super fair girl who loves to fake tan (and doesn't mind the carrot-coloured stains between her fingies). She's white grape juice that's stayed in contact with her skins and seeds. In this way, she's treated more like a red wine than a white (mashed, put in giant a vessel, left to chill with pulp still attached for four days to a year).

Funky orange grew up in Qvevri[26] in Georgia before travelling to Friuli, Italy, then Slovenia and beyond. She thinks a clear, focused mind comes from a bangin' body, so tries to consume little to no additives, even yeast. Yet this can lead to interesting (and sometimes compromising) results. People have described her as everything from bold to nutty to highly acidic to just plain sour.

Orange wine is not for everyone, so if you're feeling adventurous you'll have to seek her out from more progressive producers. In Australia, you'll find her (mostly made from Sauvignon Blanc) in SA's Mount Gambier and Adelaide Hills, Victoria's Yarra Valley and WA's Margaret River.

YOU HAD ME AT MERLOT

95

**Fave meal:** 'Don't ask me about food right now. I'm on a lemon cleanse.'

**Fave outfit:** White crochet bikini to show off that hard-won tan.

**Fave song:** 'Orange Crush' by R.E.M.

---

[26] **QVEVRI** = ceramic vessels that were sealed with beeswax and/or stone and stored underground during fermentation.

# NATURAL/ORGANIC/BIODYNAMIC/ MINIMAL INTERVENTION WINE

## Natural

Natural wine is quite an It girl right now, especially around Adelaide Hills. It's been praised for bringing in a new generation of winemakers and wine drinkers. It has an exciting reputation for both experimentation and environmental awareness. It's a promising movement that often refers to the practice of using fewer additions – fewer agrochemicals in the vineyard and fewer chemicals in the winery.

However 'natural' wine is a slightly bamboozling expression. Not everyone has the same definition for it, which is a bit of a ball ache. The term 'natural' can also be a bit of a marketing ploy[27].

The thing is, wine is not a natural product, despite using natural processes. It has to have human intervention at some juncture, whether it's in the vineyard or winery. Yet how much human intervention is too much? Can wine still be natural if it uses any sort of pesticides? If so, how much? Sulphites[28] can be naturally occurring, so what counts as a 'natural' amount?

[27] Technically, many Old World wines would also count as 'natural' because of the minimal amount of sulphites and pesticides present. They're just not marketed that way.

[28] Remember sulphites? In winemaking, this is usually in reference to 'sulphur dioxide'. Sulphites are those preservatives used to keep wine fresh and prevent oxidation. Some people (like asthma sufferers) can be more sensitive to sulphur, making organic and biodynamic wines (with less marked sulphur) quite appealing.

BECKY 'Natural' is a really slippery term because it can still be conventional fruit[29], but it might not have had much done to it. So you can pick the fruit and you process it with as little intervention as possible. A lot of them[30] choose not to add sulphur at any stage, but it's more a choice in the winery as opposed to in the vineyard.

SAM The problem is that there is no definition of what 'natural' is. It's very much up to your expectation. And that's fine as long as you don't turn around and say, 'Well, I'm natural because of this and that means you're un-natural.' Each to their own though. That's the beauty of winemaking.

AMANDA What I get tired of is when someone pours me a glass of turbid, cloudy wine that's quite tannic and then they try to explain to me why it's good. And then I have to say 'I don't need an explanation. If a wine is good, it's good.' The problem is, people are making bad wines and then trying to say, 'Well, it's natural' when it's just bad. We have some of the best ingredients in Australia in the Quay kitchen right now, but I can't go downstairs and make you a good meal. I don't have that skill. So I could go into any vineyard and say, 'This is the best fruit on earth.' But it doesn't mean I could make you a good wine.

[29] Conventional fruit refers to fruit that's not necessarily been grown organically or biodynamically.

[30] The 'them's and 'they's in this section refer to natural wine producers.

Alrighty, so to avoid the ambiguity that the term 'natural' brings up, I reckon it'll be more helpful for us to utilise terms such as organic, biodynamic and minimal intervention instead. Ready? Lessdoit. . .

## Organic

- Winemaking that avoids herbicides and fungicides, looks for sustainable alternatives
- Can still contain egg whites, animal enzymes and yeast
- 'No added sulphur' can still contain 10-40PPM of sulphur, which is markedly less than the average bottle of wine

If orange wine is a city-dwelling greenie, organic has gone full Byron Bay vegetarian on you. Organic wine is the Bikram-loving hippie who used to be a management consultant in Sydney. He's gone back to basics and is making up for lost time. He makes sure everything he produces is grown with a minimal amount of chemicals and that his child support payments are made on time.

He doesn't like to use herbicides and fungicides. Organic looks for more sustainable alternatives. He can't, however, claim that he doesn't have any additives in his system. He's not a vegan. The thing is, you can still be considered organic and contain egg whites, animal enzymes and yeast. Heck, even wines with 'no added sulphur' can contain 10 to 40PPM[31] of the good stuff. (Sulphites can be naturally occurring and you need 'em to preserve vino and keep its shelf life commercially viable.) Though organic usually does have markedly less sulphur, which is great news

31  PPM = parts per million, innit.

for drinkers with severe asthma, who are most likely to be sensitive to sulphur dioxide.

Buuuuut, remember, there's more sulphur in dried fruits than a glass of wine. Don't believe me?

**SAM** It drives me crazy when people say, 'I can't drink wine because of the sulphur levels.' I turn around and say, 'Do you eat dried apricots? Because dried apricots have like 500 times more sulphur in them than wine does.' There's a whole list of other foods that have much higher sulphur levels than wine.

In Australia, you can find organic wines from most regions. To be honest, a lot of the winemakers I've interviewed try to be as sustainable as possible anyway. They just can't guarantee that they won't use pesticides if their vines start getting a fungal infection. The difference is an organic winery has to go the whole hog. As a result the wine has the potential to lose a lot of fruit in the process. But there are some good'uns out there. My current faves are Tamburlaine in the Hunter Valley, Manon in Adelaide Hills and Momento Mori Wines in Gippsland.

YOU HAD ME AT MERLOT

99

**Fave meal:** Homemade tofu rice paper rolls.

**Fave outfit:** His elephant-patterned pants from Cambodia with the super low crotch.

**Fave song:** Anything by the John Butler Trio or Xavier Rudd.

## Biodynamic

- A more extreme form of organic winemaking
- Based on the philosophy of Rudolf Steiner
- Follows the movement of the moon and stars, uses quartz crystals and manure-stuffed cow horns (not even using hyperbole here)

Consider biodynamic as building on organic winemaking. The vegan to organic's vegetarian. She's the calm-birth-advocating earth-mother who manages to still be Type-A in ensuring her planting, growing and harvesting schedule is religiously in line with the movement of the moon and stars. She's interested in the philosophy of Rudolf Steiner and his holistic understanding of the environment. She may sound kooky with her quartz crystals and manure-stuffed cow horns, but she's very dedicated to treating the Earth as a living, receptive organism and that seems pretty refreshing in an era of melting ice caps, fracking and orange presidents.

In the land of Oz, check out Lucy Margaux in Adelaide Hills, Jauma[32] in McLaren Vale, Shobbrook Wines at Seppeltsfield in the Barossa Valley, Moon in Central Victoria, and Krinklewood Biodynamic Vineyard in the Hunter Valley. In NZ, Millton in Gisborne are rounding corners and taking names, especially for their Chardonnay and Chenin Blanc.

But it's not just smaller outfits that are going full Steiner though. Cullen Wines in Margaret River is an iconic old-school producer who

---

[32] **JAUMA** = one of the founding members of Natural Section Theory, a group of South Australian winemakers committed to sustainable and biodynamic principles, including: Anton van Klopper, Sam Hughes, James Erskine and Tom Shobbrook.

grows biodynamic fruit. I heart Vanya Cullen's wines. They're so bright you can almost feel them humming with life.

**AMANDA** Her wines are exceptional, but she does plenty of entry-level wines and they're all biodynamic fruit. She's religious in following the moon, tides, biodynamic calendar to the nth degree.

> **Fave meal:** A nourishing casserole, made from veggies from her own garden.
>
> **Fave outfit:** A vintage kaftan and clunky, Iris Apfel-esque bangles.
>
> **Fave song:** An impromptu fireside jam sesh.

YOU HAD ME AT MERLOT

## Minimal intervention

- Uses largely sustainable practices
- Still open to using sulphur and cultured yeasts
- Prioritises terroir over winemaker's imprint

Minimal intervention is my future husband. He's woke, yet uber practical. He has a real sense of place and an awareness of his environment. Major babe. But it doesn't mean he's all weirdy-beardy-absolutely-no-additives-no-sirree-bob.

Our resident expert Samantha uses minimal intervention processes at Stargazer Wine (including my personal fave Tupelo

Pinot Gris/Riesling/Gewurtztraminer blend). She attributes a lot of her success to her southern Tasmanian location . . .

 **SAM** The fruit balance in Tasmania is such that I don't have to intervene much. And from a winemaking perspective that's really what we're all aiming for - to get our viticulture right and to have our vineyards in the right spot, so that we don't need to add this, that and the other to make the wine balanced. Once the fruit is right, you don't have to stuff around as a winemaker. That's what minimal intervention is about to me - letting the fruit express itself, making sure that it expresses the vineyard, that is expresses the site. It's not expressing the imprint of the winemaker.

## TRUE OR FALSE Is sulphur the Devil's preservative?

Okay, this is a fairly contentious topic in the wine world. Winemakers traditionally add sulphur dioxide ($SO_2$) after racking[33] to preserve wine from bacterial spoilage and oxidation. Many consider it crucial to ensure quality and consistency in their wines.

However, $SO_2$ has recently received a bad reputation amongst asthmatics and those who blame the preservative for their hangovers. But the thing is, while us asthmatics are more prone to sulphite intolerance, adverse reactions are extremely rare. And in regards to your hangover, it's probs the alcohol not the sulphites that are making you wish you were dead.

[33] **RACKING** = to siphon wine off from one container to the next, leaving sediment behind.

Too much sulphur dioxide can mute a wine's flavours though, like in a lot of cask wines. So looking up minimal intervention producers or seeking out labels with 'minimal sulphites' is a pretty safe bet when considering 'To sulphur or not to sulphur?' (Though if you do find an experienced producer who can pull off the high-wire act of using no added sulphur at all, by all means, drink up!)

**SAM** I agree with the concept of trying to reduce the amount of sulphur in winemaking, but I love sulphur. I think it does an amazing job from a winemaking point of view. And I don't like faulty wine. I think that says more about the winemaker than the fruit. We shouldn't give people faulty wine and expect them to enjoy it. Pretty controversial topic.

On the hunt for this legend? There are so many good minimal intervention wines in Australia + NZ. Where do I start?

YOU HAD ME AT MERLOT

Bloodwood, Orange
- Use minimal sulphur additions.

Commune of Buttons, Adelaide Hills
- Transitioning into organic and biodynamic practices.

Domaine Simha, Simla & Sanskrit, Tasmania
- Methods they embrace include harvesting by lunar cycle and whole bunch wild fermentation.

Don Wines, Nelson, Martinborough and Hawke's Bay
- Work with both certified and uncertified organic vineyards.

Ochota Barrels, Adelaide Hills
- Becky thinks his wines are fantastic: 'Seamless and bright'

Tarrington Vineyards, Henty
- Use biodynamic farming practices and minimal preservatives.

Unico Zelo
- The brainchild of winemakers Brendan and Laura Carter. Based in Adelaide Hills. Specialise in Italian varieties like Fiano, Nebbiolo, Dolcetto, and Nero D'avola.

**Fave meal:** If only I knew, I'd break my 'no cooking' rule and learn how to make it for him.

**Fave outfit:** Again if only I knew. He'd be so much easier to spot in a crowd.

**Fave song:** The chicken dance song. (Or something equally surprising/refreshing.)

## ROSÉ

So heads up, there is no rosé grape. Rosé is the result of a winemaking method, not a pink ball of goodness. For example, Pinot Noir grapes can be use to create white, red and rosé, as can Grenache, Syrah and Sangiovese.

The majority of rosés get their colour from having limited contact with red grape skins. The length of contact is determined by the winemaker. That's why rosés range in colour from blush pink to dark peach and with flavours from strawberries and cream to rose petal to honey dew. The whole venture is basically a mixture of red and white winemaking techniques. But but but, very rarely is it a combo of red and white wine. Weirdly common misconception. This ain't pre-school and we ain't mixing paint. This type of blending technique sometimes happens in sparkling wine regions like Champagne, but barely anywhere else.

I genuinely didn't think I liked rosé until earlier this year when I tasted a dry, savoury one from Provence. But further research (drinking) has made me realise how great Aussie rosé can be. According to Amanda, South Australia used to be famous for using its excess fruit to make incredible rosé.

However, now, there are great rosé producers all across the country, including:

- De Iuliis Grenache Rosé, Hunter Valley
- Golden Ball, Beechworth
- Seville Estate, Yarra Valley

*you HAD me AT MERLOT*

Tim reckons it's because rosé suits the Aussie climate really well. Our winemakers are also prone to playful experimentation with compelling results. . .

**TIM** A lot of winemakers have been playing around with extended maceration. That's why some of our rosés blur that line between what's a rosé and what's a chilled light red.

My personal faves are:

- The super savoury, biodynamic 2016 Hochkirch Maceration rosé from Victoria
- Deviation Road sparkling rosé (and white) from Adelaide Hills
- It's not Aussie, but Grenache-based rosés from Southern Rhône, France, are pretty delish and pair oh so well with food

The more common methods for making rosé include:

## HOT TIP

The flavour of a rosé depends more on what grape varieties have been used and where it's been grown, than how it's been made. Though the method can help make varietal characteristics pop out a bit more.

## HOT TIP

To avoid a sickly sweet rosé, look for one with a pale tone. The paler the rosé, the drier the rosé. You will rarely find a dark rosé that is dry.

## Direct Press

- Method for making rosé in which red grapes are treated like white wine grapes
- Minimal contact with grapes, resulting in lighter colour
- Popular in France, particularly Provence and Languedoc-Roussillon

Rosé made with this method is like that guy who's fair in winter, but can get stupidly bronzed in summer. He's great at catching colour: it can take him only a couple of hours to get that rosé-glow. All he has to do is rest in his own juices before his whole body is transformed. He's popular in France, particularly Languedoc-Roussillon and Provence, where he's just as beloved as his red and white brothers and sisters. He's known for charming aromatics and slightly more delicate flavours.

Fave meal: Salt and pepper squid.

Fave outfit: Camel-coloured shorts. No shirt.

Fave song: 'God is a DJ' by Pink.

## Saignée

- Method for making rosé that's more common in the US and beyond
- Uses must[34] siphoned off during red winemaking process
- *Saignée* = 'to bleed' in French

Rosé made by the Saignée ('son-yay') method is like that one girl in a family of super boy-sy boys. She's the younger sister who gets shuffled away from the rest of red wine family to do deportment classes while her brothers play football. She could be part of the high quality table wine family, but her parents have other hopes for her. According to Amanda, she usually has three to eighteen hours of skin contact. I guess she's a modern day Cinderella — beautiful, but thwarted from going to the ball (or is that from playing with the ball?)

*you HAD me AT MERLOT*

[34]  **MUST** = what you get when you crush a bunch of grapes. Includes all the juice and pulp of the stems, skins and seeds.

Saignée (or 'Bled') Rosé mostly hangs around the US, especially Napa and Sonoma, California. She doesn't get quite the same prestige she does in France, but she can turn it out with ripe flavours and lively expression of varietal.

**Fave meal:** Spicy Indian cuisine.

**Fave outfit:** Much prefers an oversized tee, leggings and hi-top sneaks to the trim '50s silhouettes her step-mum picks out for her.

**Fave song:** 'A Dream is a Wish Your Heart Makes' from Disney's *Cinderella*.

## SPARKLING

We've all done it – we've asked for a glass of *Champagne* when we mean *sparkling*. But then the real Champagne in France was like, 'Hey, stop that' and got litigious about other people using their good name. That shizz has been trademarked under the Madrid system since 1891 and further protected by the EU since the 90s, so that even *Champagne method* and *Methode Champenoise* are off-limits on sparkling labels.

Because of that, most countries have adopted their own word (and cheat codes) for sparkling. Italy has *Spumante*, Spain has *Cava*, South Africa has *Sekt*. Outside of Champagne, French regions Alsace and Burgundy produce *Crémant*.

So how best to differentiate the many, many different types? Let's imagine sparkling wine like a big reality TV family. Let's imagine the sparkling wine production methods as the Kardashians. Let's keep up with them.

## On Champagne in reality shows

BEN    Have you ever watched any of *The Real Housewives* franchise? The Auckland one is amazing. I think part of it is funny because it's Auckland and what the fuck is this? But one of the women there is Anne the Champagne Lady. Her job is she trades in Champagne and she's quite amazingly haughty about it - how you have to hold the stem, how to hold the glass is a huge violation. But she's got this incredible room in her house. It's essentially a cold room just for Champagne. Yeah, watch it.

YOU
HAD
ME
AT
MERLOT

## Classic Method

- Uses most famous method, *Methode Traditionnelle*
- Originated in Champagne, very protective of its brand
- Secondary fermentation happens within the bottle

109

All sparkling wines go through two fermentation processes. However, Classic Method would be the Kim Kardashian of sparkling – the most famous and fashionable. She makes the others famous by association. Classic is linked with Champagne, Cava and other sparklings that imitate the Champagne style (*Methode Traditionnelle*). She has finer, longer-lasting bubbles (and a more iconic career to boot).

Much like Kim post-Paris robbery, Classic Method is more protective of herself and her reputation. And unlike her more open sister Charmat, her second fermentation happens privately (that is, inside the bottle) before a process of disgorgement (removing excess yeast, sometimes adding sugar).

**Fave meal:** Salmon caviar on hard-boiled eggs.

**Fave outfit:** A sheer, couture dress á la Kim K's Met Ball Gala dress circa 2015.

**Fave song:** Nicki Minaj's part in Kanye's 'Monster'.

## Charmat Method
- Second-most-famous method, known for producing big, explosive bubbles
- Made famous by Prosecco and Lambrusco
- Secondary fermentation happens in large steel tanks

Charmat (AKA the Italian, AKA Tank) Method is the outspoken, younger sister of the group. The Khloé. If Charmat could have another TV show she would. She's bigger and more explosive in her bubbliness. She's responsible for Prosecco[35], Lambrusco and other lightly sparkling wines.

---

[35] Heads up, King Valley in Victoria does some mean Prosecco.

Charmat doesn't contain her second fermentation to the bottle. She makes sure it happens in the open, in big, steel pressure tanks where yeast and sugar can be easily added. She can be produced at a slightly lower cost, but – HOOH MAMA – she's fun to have around.

Fave meal: Fried chicken on cheat days.

Fave outfit: Grey leotard á la *Revenge Body with Khloé Kardashian* reality show.

Fave song: Something to dance to. 'Formation' by Beyoncé.

## Continuous Method

- Lesser known method of making sparkling wine
- Secondary fermentation happens in steel tanks, where wine is encouraged to circulate
- Popular in Russia and Ukraine

YOU HAD ME AT MERLOT

Continuous (or Russian) Method is the tiny Kourtney of sparkling techniques – not as well-known and always moving. Like Kourtney running after her three kids, Continuous Method's second fermentation happens in steel tanks where the wine is encouraged to circulate constantly. She'll be pushed and shoved through many tanks filled with wood shavings to collect dead yeast cells. Sounds icky, tastes delicious. She's incredibly popular in Russia and Ukraine.

**Fave meal:** At her sweetest, she cuts through a Sichuan spicy hot pot like whoa.

**Fave outfit:** Anything red from the Kardashians' D-A-S-H clothing boutique.

**Fave song:** 'Work' by Rihanna.

---

## Cheat guide to how sweet your champers will be

**Brut Nature:** Driest of the dry.

**Extra Brut:** Extra dry.

**Brut:** Dry.

**Extra Dry/Extra Sec:** Weirdly means just an itty bit sweet.

**Dry/Sec:** Sweet.

**Demi-Sec:** Even more sweet.

**Doux:** Sweetest of the sweet. Reaching for K-Pop levels of sweetness.

## Super happy fun task for winos

Interested in experimenting with some new styles of vino? List the
top three styles or producers you want to add to your bucket list.

1. _____

_____

2. _____

_____

3. _____

_____

YOU
HAD
ME
AT
MERLOT

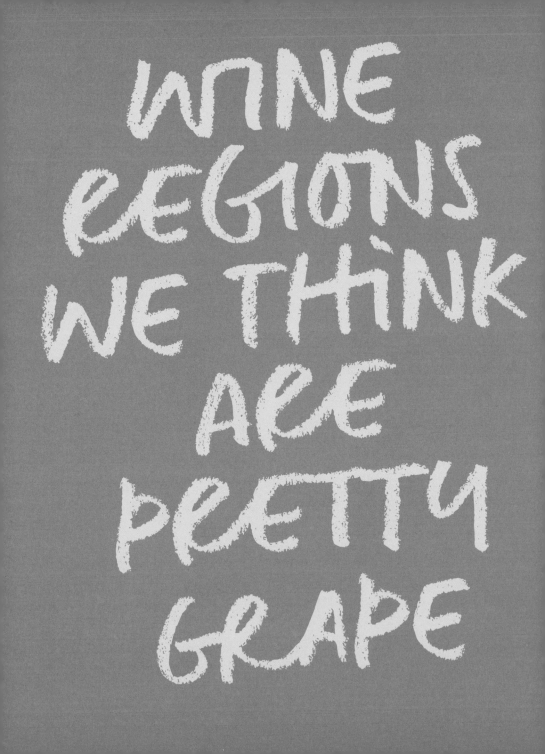

'I DRANK A QUEENSLAND
WINE RECENTLY THAT
WAS TOTALLY FINE AND I'M
JUST LIKE, "WHAT IS THIS?
WHAT'S GOING ON?"
I FELT DECEIVED, BUT
IT WAS ACTUALLY
PRETTY DELICIOUS.'

Benjamin Law

**HAVE YOU HEARD PEOPLE SAY** we live in a golden age of television? Well, if you live in Australia or New Zealand, you are basically living in a golden age of winemaking, too. It's like *The Sopranos* meets *The Wire* up in here. There is award-winning shizz as far as the eye can see.

**AMANDA** We have amazing wines in Australia. We're going through a renaissance in our wine industry right now and the rest of the world really hasn't caught on to what we have.

So get a jump-start on the rest of the globe and discover which rad wines you can find in your very own backyard. Getting familiar with Aussie and Kiwi regions is not only an easy way to bump up your vino knowledge, it's great inspo for your next freaky weekend away. Let's have a topline look at each state, their highest-exporting/travel-worthy regions, and what moreish vino you can put in your mouth.

WINE REGIONS WE THINK ARE PRETTY GRAPE

# GUESS WHERE?
## (THE WINE EDITION)

Want to lose friends and alienate people? Play a game of 'Guess where?' with your wine club. It's like 'Guess who?' with fewer moustaches. Winner gets to take home all the remaining vinos and a crown of glory.

**Step One:** Take a gander at a map of Australia and New Zealand.

**Step Two:** Get one person to name an Aussie or Kiwi wine region they know.

**Step Three:** Everyone else guesses where aforementioned wine region is located.

**Step Four:** The furthest from the region is a loser-y loser who gets cut from the game.

**Step Five:** Repeat process, cutting one person at a time from the game in a *Hunger Games*-style game of geography.

**Step Six:** The last two contestants compete in a sudden-death match until someone cooks it and a winner is declared.

# AUSTRALIA

## WESTERN AUSTRALIA

### Greater Perth
### Swan District (in particular, Swan Valley)
First People Tribal/Language Group[1]: Wajuk
### Known for:
- Chardonnay
- Chenin Blanc
- Verdelho
- Shiraz

[1]   Information based off AIATSIS map of Aboriginal Australia. More detailed information can be obtained from their online database of Australian Indigenous languages (AUSTLANG) or by contacting the National Native Title Tribunal.

Follow the scenic 32-kilometre Swan Valley Food & Wine Trail and sample a buttery Chardonnay, lush Chenin Blanc and honeyed Verdelho. Keep an eye out for the Upper Reach cellar door, where Shiraz is king. Tell them Grace sent you. (Actually, don't. They don't know who I am.)

## South West Australia
### (including Geographe, Great Southern & Margaret River)

*MICHAEL* South West Australia is unique in that it's influenced by both the warmer Indian Ocean and the much cooler Southern Ocean, resulting in many sub-regions with unique microclimates and terroirs. The best thing is that multiple varieties grow well and produce great wines here, not just one or two varieties.

### Geographe
First People Tribal/Language Group: Wardandi and Kaniyang
Known for:

- Cabernet Sauvignon
- Sauvignon Blanc
- Semillon
- Shiraz

Most peeps think Margaret River when they think Western Australian wine. But don't forget Geographe and its diverse collection of boutique producers. Elegant Cabernet Sauvignon grows a treat here, as does Sauvignon Blanc (ranging from lemony to melony), tangy Semillon, and Shiraz that can vary from delicate to meaty.

When you need a break from wine tasting, take a hike by the Collie River in Wellington National Park. And if you're into scuba, pack your flippiest of flippers and head to the Lena Wreck in Bunbury. It's a giant fishing boat that was purposefully sunk in 2003, after being apprehended by the Aussie Navy. Suitable for Open Water Divers and those hunting for sunken treasure.

## Great Southern

First People Tribal/Language Group: Minang

Known for:

- Riesling
- Chardonnay
- Cabernet Sauvignon
- Shiraz

One of the most southwest of the southwest region – Great Southern stretches across Denmark, Mount Barker and Albany and is considered by road-trippers to be 'the tits'[2]. It's known for its intense Riesling and, more recently, its elegant Chardonnay, classic Cabernet Sauvignon and spicy Shiraz.

If you're road-tripping from Margaret River, pleaaaaase check out the Gloucester Tree in the Gloucester National Park on your way there. It's a giant karri tree that is the world's second tallest fire-lookout. At over 58 metres high, it is not for everyone. So don't feel bad if you don't make it all the way to the top. Most peeps just have a quick squizz from halfway then hustle their way back down like two possums on a powerline.

[2]   I should definitely not be quoting this. No one has ever said this ever.

WINE
REGIONS
WE
THINK
ARE
PRETTY
GRAPE

## Margaret River

First People Tribal/Language Group: Wardandi

Known for:

- Cabernet Sauvignon
- Chardonnay
- Semillon

Aussie and international winos froth for Margaret River. And for good reason. Margaret River is where intense Chardonnay and full-bodied Cabernet Sauvignon thrive, thanks to its Bordeaux-like climate. Located southwest of Perth, it's that 'only in Australia' combo of pretty wineries next to surf beaches and national parks.

So a super-happy-fun-time there could literally involve learning to surf in the morning and drinking a crisp Semillon in the afternoon.

Margaret River is a great base for exploring one of Australia's premium winegrowing states. Foodies should head there in November for the four-day Margaret River Gourmet Escape festival and nom on all the truffles, berries, chocolate, cheese and fudge on offer. (Just don't go swimming straight after, mate.)

## SOUTH AUSTRALIA

### Barossa (including Barossa Valley & Eden Valley)

### Barossa Valley
First People Tribal/Language Group: Peramangk
**Known for:**
- Shiraz
- Cabernet Sauvignon
- Riesling

For ripe, full-bodied Shiraz, rich Cabernet Sauvignon, and limy Riesling, head east from Adelaide to the Barossa Valley. September to November is the best time to visit for you closet wildflower enthusiasts. (You know who you are!)

Unlike the blossoms, wine is perennial here. Blend your own wine at the Penfolds Barossa Valley Cellar Door or – for something less interactive – park yourself at the Birdwood Cheese and Wine Centre in Tanunda and get all of the local produce in ya.

### Eden Valley

First People Tribal/Language Group: Peramangk

Known for:

- Riesling
- Shiraz

Eden Valley is more than just a cool climate with a pretty face. This is where Riesling comes to show off its lime aromas with some intense flavours. James Halliday lives for Eden Valley Rieslings. Their plummy Shiraz is on point too, particularly the world-renowned Hill of Grace.

    After you've visited Taste Eden Valley (a collaborative cellar door, featuring many of the region's most impressive wines under one roof), take yourself on a bushwalk through Kaiserstuhl Conservation Park, nestled within the Barossa Ranges. You're bound to see some kangaroos rounding corners and taking names. (Not literally, that would be weird.)

WINE REGIONS WE THINK ARE PRETTY GRAPE

123

### Mount Lofty Ranges

(including Adelaide Hills & Clare Valley)

### Adelaide Hills

First People Tribal/Language Group: Peramangk

Known for:

- Sauvignon Blanc
- Pinot Noir
- Minimal intervention wines

Less than forty-five minutes' drive from Adelaide, chilly-willy Adelaide Hills produces some mean Sauvignon Blanc. Alongside Margaret River and Orange, it's one of Oz's biggest Sauvy producers and the epicentre of Oz's minimal intervention wine scene. Expect tropical yet ballsy wine with real power and structure. Unlike other South Australian regions, Adelaide Hills is known for being cooler in climate and better suited to early ripening varieties. So strap yourself in for a medium-bodied Pinot Noir with ripe cherry flavours (and make sure you pack a beanie/scarf/animal-onesie combo).

 **TIM** Places like Adelaide Hills - which is slightly elevated, so wines are not necessarily as concentrated or as heavy - are real wine hotspots, especially in the natural wine scene. There's a lot happening up there.

 **BECKY** Adelaide Hills is kicking goals. So many legends down there, like Anton van Klopper from Domaine Lucci, and Lucy Margaux. Then there's James Erskine from Jauma. It's a beautiful community.

While you're there, pick your own strawberries and cherries at the local orchards. You can even cuddle a koala at Gorge Wildlife Park in Cudlee Creek (you cannot make this stuff up). And for real culture vultures, start the car 'cause the Big Rocking Horse is in nearby Gumeracha, and we need to get there yesterday.

## Clare Valley

First People Tribal/Language Group: Ngadjuri

**Known for:**

- Riesling
- Cabernet Sauvignon
- Shiraz

North of the Barossa you'll find the Clare Valley and its iconic, age-worthy[3] Rieslings. In May, you can catch the annual Clare Valley Gourmet Weekend and smash local food and wine like the Cookie Monster on a biscuit bender.

If you find yourself there outside of May, don't fret, pet. Cycle the Riesling Trail[4] from Auburn to Clare, stopping off at cellar doors along the way. Yeah, it's thirty-five kilometres if you ride it all the way to Barinia, but there are also three loop trails you can choose if you don't want to circle back and get into a fight with your girlfriend about who left your water bottle at which winery. Plus, it's an easy journey with a very gentle gradient, so you won't need to wear high-vis lycra and/or an aerodynamic helmet.

*WINE REGIONS WE THINK ARE PRETTY GRAPE*

125

## Limestone Coast Zone

**(including Coonawarra & Mount Gambier)**

### Coonawarra[5]

First People Tribal/Language Group: no published information available. Potentially Buandig or Bindjali.

---

[3] **AGE-WORTHY** = improves in quality and taste through ageing.

[4] Go to rieslingtrail.com.au for more deets.

[5] **COONAWARRA** = an Indigenous word for 'honeysuckle'.

Known for:

- Cabernet Sauvignon
- Shiraz
- Merlot
- Riesling

With its first grapevines being planted in 1891, those who love Cabernet Sauvignon will adore Coonawarra . Its beloved terra rossa soil offers great balance to the vines that grow upon it. Think soil that stores and drains water like a boss. So it's not surprising that the town has earned acclaim for having Australia's most famous terroir – their dirt and climate be famous, y'all.

Coonawarra also can produce silken, cool-climate offerings of spicy Shiraz, Merlot that blends oh so well with Cabernet, and floral Riesling. When you're not visiting cellar doors like Redman Wines, Leconfield, Raidis Estate or the three-gabled Wynns Coonawarra Estate, make sure you eat, drink and antique your way through neighbouring Penola. From personal experience, their bakery does a tear-jerkingly good vanilla slice.

## Mount Gambier

First People Tribal/Language Group: Buandig

Known for:

- Pinot Noir
- Sauvignon Blanc
- Chardonnay
- Pinot Gris

Mount Gambier is known for its Mediterranean climate, volcanic activity, rock lobsters and producing moreish Pinot Noir, Sauvignon Blanc, Chardonnay and Pinot Gris. You know what else it's known for? A sinkhole. Let me be more specific – the Umpherston Sinkhole.

Otherwise known as the Sunken Garden, it's a surprisingly stunning park created inside a collapsed limestone cave. Plus, if you come between December and March you can see the natural wonder of the Blue Lake, a volcanic crater lake that turns cobalt in the summer. (I want to go to there.)

## Fleurieu
## (including Langhorne Creek & McLaren Vale)

## Langhorne Creek

First People Tribal/Language Group: Ngarrindjeri

Known for:

- Cabernet Sauvignon
- Shiraz

WINE REGIONS WE THINK ARE PRETTY GRAPE

127

Toasty warm Langhorne Creek is the little wine region that could. Its special skillz are easy-drinking Cabernet Sauvignon with big, red berry flavours, and equally fruity Shiraz. Langhorne Creek is one of our oldest wine regions and a nice day trip from Adelaide (under an hour's drive away).

For a freaky weekend that'll set your heart racing, try skydiving from 9000, 12,000 or 15,000 feet while you're there. Who said weekends spent wine tasting were all about unwinding?

## McLaren Vale

First People Tribal/Language Group: Kaurna
**Known for:**
- Shiraz
- Chardonnay
- Vermentino
- Fiano

With over sixty vineyards, McLaren Vale has a reputation as one of SA's ooh la la, so very fancy premier wine regions. Think warm country town known for being a Leviathan-sized producer of fruity Shiraz, various styles of Chardonnay and experimenting with new guys like Vermentino[6] and Fiano[7].

You know what it also has? Wine tours on Harley-Davidsons. Not even kidding. All I want for Christmas is a ride through the vines with McLaren Vale Motorcycle Tours.

[6]  **VERMENTINO** = a dry, light-bodied white wine varietal, originally from the island of Sardinia in Italy.

[7]  **FIANO** = a rich, strongly flavoured white wine varietal from southern Italy.

# NORTHERN TERRITORY

Not really a thing when it comes to grape-growing. Great to visit, not an intuitive place to grow vineyards. Sweltering humidity and extreme wet seasons do not a wine region make[8].

# QUEENSLAND

### Granite Belt

First People Tribal/Language Group: Ngarabal

Known for:

* Alternative varieties, for example, Barbera, Durif, Gewürztraminer, Marsanne, Mourvèdre, Pinot Gris, Tempranillo and Viognier

WINE REGIONS WE THINK ARE PRETTY GRAPE

Call me sheltered, but I genuinely did not know that Queensland had a wine industry until recently. Centred around the town of Stanthorpe, Granite Belt has over fifty wineries and a growing reputation for innovating with alternative varieties. To be considered 'alternative', the varietal has to count for less than 1% of vines in Australia, as defined by Wine Australia. That is, wines that aren't the usual suspects like Cabernet Sauvignon, Shiraz, Chardonnay, Riesling and Pinot Noir.

Think instead of mofos like Barbera, Durif, Gewürztraminer, Marsanne, Mourvèdre[9], Pinot Gris, Tempranillo and Viognier. In Queensland, they refer to them as Strange Birds.

---

[8]   Though places like Bali and Thailand are actually giving winemaking a crack nowadays. And good luck to 'em.

[9]   Haven't heard of any of these varieties? There's a lot there, I know, too many to pack into a footnotes section. But don't stress, this is a great opportunity to try each of them for yourself!

Drive yourself off the beaten track — both physically and figuratively — as you make your way along the Strange Bird Alternative Wine Trail. It's like a treasure hunt for Australia's most obscure wines. *The Amazing Race* for winos.

**BEN** I drank a Queensland wine recently that was totally fine and I'm just like, 'What is this? What's going on? Granite Belt – that doesn't even sound like Queensland.' I felt deceived, but it was actually pretty delicious.

## ACT

See below, bud.

# NEW SOUTH WALES

### Canberra District[10]

First People Tribal/Language Group: Ngunawal

Known for:

- Shiraz
- Riesling

For elegant, cool-climate Shiraz and damn fine Riesling, pack the car because we are going to the Canberra District. This is the perfect tranquil weekend getaway

[10]  I know, I know, it sounds like it should be ACT, but it's not technically in Canberra. It comprises over thirty wineries that are thirty-five minutes to an hour's drive north of Canberra's CBD.

for foodies. Not only does the region have beautiful wine and a distant view of the Snowy Mountains, it's rife with truffles. RIFE.

Visit during June or August for The Truffle Festival and kill two delicious birds with one stone. But remember, Canberra's temperature can range from very, VERY cold nights to hot summer days, so pack with an eye on your weather app and a hand on your lover.

## Central Ranges (in particular, Mudgee)

### Mudgee

First People Tribal/Language Group: Wiradjuri

Known for:

- Cabernet Sauvignon
- Chardonnay
- Semillon

Pretty gal Mudgee (meaning 'Nest in the Hills') is encircled by a ring of hills and really can be as warm and snugly bugly as a bird's nest. Top varieties to taste there include tannin-heavy Cabernet Sauvignon, Chardonnay with flavours of peach, fig and melon, as well as cellar-worthy Semillon.

It has over forty family-owned cellar doors, a food-and-wine festival in September and hot air ballooning. Let me repeat that. Hot. Air. Ballooning. Sign me up for a breakfast of sparkling and stunning valley views plz.

WINE REGIONS WE THINK ARE PRETTY GRAPE

## Hunter Valley

First People Tribal/Language Group: Wonnarua and Wiradjuri

**Known for:**

- Semillon
- Shiraz
- Chardonnay

A trip to the humid Hunter is a trip to Australia's oldest wine region. With over 120 cellar doors, you will be spoiled for choice when it comes to wetting your whistle. It's known for producing bold, world-class Semillon and Shiraz, but don't look past their various styles of Chardonnay either. It's also known for the Upper and Lower Hunter Valleys' wariness of each other. Much sibling rivalry, very *Lion King*.

**TIM**  There's great wine coming out of there. It's a very big region and there is an element of mass production up there, but there are also some great producers.

Upper Hunter (including Muswellbrook, Pokolbin and Hawkesbury) has a rep for being more of a boutique clique, even going so far as to have its own separate website. But whether you're visiting Upper or Lower Hunter, make sure you do yourself a favour and avoid driving: book a minibus or hire a bike and wobble your way through the afternoon. Très *Call the Midwife*. (Don't get that reference? Neither do I. I just saw the cover of the series box-set where the women are all on bikes looking happy and I thought it was cute.)

## Orange

First People Tribal/Language Group: Wiradjuri

**Known for:**

- Chardonnay
- Shiraz
- Sauvignon Blanc

About three-and-a-half hours' drive from Sydney, cool-calm-collected Orange and its rich volcanic soils is known for Chardonnay, fragrant Shiraz and tropical Sauvignon Blanc at higher elevations.

You know what else this beautiful region produces? Sheeeeeeps' cheese so good it'll make you happy-cry (as well as some lush stone fruits). Visit in October if you want to catch the Orange Wine Festival, including night markets, local produce, and plenty of free wine tastings. (Orange you glad I told you about it? See what I did there? See what I . . . yeah.)

WINE REGIONS WE THINK ARE PRETTY GRAPE

## Riverina

First People Tribal/Language Group: Wiradjuri

**Known for:**

- Chardonnay
- Semillon

If you've ever claimed you hate Chardonnay, it's probably because of the Riverina (and the Hunter Valley). Let me unpack that. In the 80s, the Riverina exported intensely oak-chipped Chardonnay like it was any old movie script and they were Nicolas Cage. The Riverina's sunshiny disposition and status as the largest wine-producing region in New South Wales meant it got a bloated, commercial rep. However, it has developed a strong food-and-wine culture that shouldn't be overlooked. If Chardonnay is really not your thing, try their Semillon – both as a table and dessert wine.

Griffith is the centre of this uber flat, uber dry region. If you go in October, you'll be just in time for their Spring Fest, featuring more than seventy citrus sculptures. That is, giant sculptures covered in oranges. Because YOLO.

# VICTORIA

## Central Victoria

First People Tribal/Language Group: Djadjawurung, Baraba Baraba, Ngurraiillam and Taungurong
Known for:
- Chardonnay
- Shiraz
- Pinot Noir

When you think Central Victoria, think Mount Macedon, Woodend, Daylesford, Heathcote and Bendigo. Woodend, right in the centre of the Macedon Ranges, is a solid base for your wino travels, but Daylesford is where lavender lovers should run (not walk). A weekend there could legit include a stroll through Lavandula Swiss Italian Farm, sampling wines from the neighbouring hills, Sunday farmers' markets and a soak in restorative mineral springs. (If anyone wants to date me, please note that this is what I would like to do next weekend.)

Keep an eye out for their sparkling wine, as well as their elegant Chardonnay, Shiraz and Pinot Noir. The cool climate combined with the high elevation lends itself well to these varieties, producing a moreish, silken wine. Translation: iz good.

## Gippsland

First People Tribal/Language Group: Kurnai

**Known for:**

- Pinot Noir
- Chardonnay
- Cabernet Sauvignon
- Merlot

WINE REGIONS WE THINK ARE PRETTY GRAPE

135

Located southeast of Melbourne, Gippsland covers a huge expanse of picturesque coastlines and Insta-worthy hillsides. Come for the views, stay for the family-owned wineries.

The Pinot Noir here should be your first order of business. Once again, cool climate lends itself really well to this varietal and while styles tend to vary throughout the region, south Gippsland has the loudest reputation for elegant Pinot with great length. You can also find some really balanced, easy-drinking Chardonnay in west Gippsland.

And if you want to live out your Batman fantasies while you're in the area, take a day-trip to the Buchan Caves and tour the underground limestone formations, created over 400 million years ago. BYO Batsuit.

**Port Phillip** (including Mornington Peninsula & Yarra Valley)

### Mornington Peninsula

First People Tribal/Language Group: Boonwurrung

Known for:

- Pinot Noir
- Chardonnay
- Pinot Gris

Mornington Peninsula is a great freaky weekend destination in April and May when the autumn leaves are ON POINT. Plus, there's the Peninsula Hot Springs with a view of the ocean (from the top pool) and award-winning Pinot Noir and olive oil to fill your car boot with. Their Chardonnay and Pinot Gris is also pretty bangin' (especially from family-run Mooroduc Estate, who also make their own moreish bread).

### Yarra Valley

First People Tribal/Language Group: Woiworung

Known for:

- Pinot Noir
- Cabernet Sauvignon
- Chardonnay

Yarra Valley (AKA Victoria's first wine region) is known as one of Australia's premium winegrowing regions, home to world-renowned brands like St Huberts, De Bortoli and Oakridge Wines.

Pinot Noir grows super well in the region, usually light to medium-bodied with sucker punches of cherry, plum and strawberry flavours. Cabernet Sauvignon also works a treat here and Chardonnay is often very elegant, thanks to the region's natural chilly-willy-ness.

If you go during summer, take a dip in the Yarra River near the Big Peninsula Tunnel. The tunnel was hand-dug during the Gold Rush to divert the river. Now it's a rad spot to cool off and picnic near. Get amongst it. (Though maybz don't mix swimming with wine-tasting.)

## Northeast Victoria (including Beechworth & Rutherglen)

### Beechworth

First People Tribal/Language Group: Waveroo

Known for:

- Chardonnay
- Shiraz
- Pinot Noir

WINE REGIONS WE THINK ARE PRETTY GRAPE

137

Three hours' drive northeast of Melbourne, Beechworth is a small gold-rush town with mineral-rich soils that punches well above its weight. Expect big, intense Chardonnay, earthy Shiraz and medium-bodied Pinot Noir with a cherry vibe.

If you go in October, you'll not only experience hilltop picnic spots, idyllic waterfalls and all of the noms, you can also compete in The Barrowthon. Competitors recreate a bet made in 1935 and push a wheelbarrow eighty-eight kilometres from Beechworth to Mount Buffalo, raising funds for a charity of their choice. (You CANNOT make this stuff up.)

## Rutherglen

First People Tribal/Language Group: Waveroo

Known for:

- Fortified wines
- Durif[11]
- Muscat
- Marsanne
- Muscadelle
- Chardonnay
- Shiraz

Located in northeast Victoria near the New South Wales border, the small town of Rutherglen is known for striking gold and liquid gold (that's a fortified wine reference for those of you playing at home). Its warm days and cool nights mean a range of varieties flourish here, including Durif, Muscat, Marsanne, Muscadelle (Tokay) and more traditional varieties like Chardonnay and Shiraz. And if you're into antiques (in particular, creepy porcelain dolls who are dead behind the eyes), make sure you deck it here on the last weekend of August for the Antique Fair in neighbouring Chiltern.

---

[11] **DURIF** = this powerful red varietal has come up a few times, so it's probably worth mentioning. It's dark, with hints of cedar and similarities to Nebbiolo.

# TASMANIA

First People Tribal/Language Group: Peerapper, Tommeginne, Pyemmairrener, Tyerrernotepanner, Lairmairrener, Toogee, Paredarerme and Nuenonne

Known for:

- Sparkling wine
- Riesling
- Pinot Noir

Tassie for me is all about the sparkling – Jansz Premium Cuvée, Pirie, Heemskerk and House of Arras are my current beloveds. Thanks to its idyllic cool climate, this region is the Aussie wine industry's 'one to watch' (and just a bloody beautiful place to hike/hide away).

Tassie also makes a mean Riesling and Pinot Noir. And oysters. The oysters here are OH SO tasty. Plus, MONA, amirite? Come for Hobart's Museum of Old and New Art and its darkly sexy exhibitions, stay for the wine and noms.

WINE
REGIONS
WE
THINK
ARE
PRETTY
GRAPE

139

TIM  The major [wine-growing] areas are in the north like Tamar Valley, which is just outside of Launceston, and then in the south there's Upper Derwent (north of Hobart). Then you've got small pockets in areas like the Huon Valley.

There's been a lot of interest from mainland producers who have moved down there to work with cool climate wines. Climate-wise, they resonate more with what we have seen coming out of New Zealand in the last ten, twenty years.

# NEW ZEALAND

There are more than twelve wine regions and sub-regions extending over 1600 kilometres of New Zealand. I wish I had the word count to tell you how brilliant Gisborne, Wairarapa, Nelson, Canterbury and North Canterbury, Waitaki Valley (North Otago), Bay of Plenty, Waikato and Northland are. But alas, I do not. So instead, let's focus in on four major regions and why you definitely need to get their wine inside you.

## NORTH ISLAND

### Auckland (in particular, Waiheke Island)
Māori region[12]: Tāmaki and Hauraki
Known for:
- Syrah
- Pinot Gris

As one of NZ's oldest regions, Auckland is sprawling and diverse, offering both boutique wineries alongside large commercial ones. If you're looking for a memorable North Island day trip – or better yet, a weekend away – I couldn't recommend Waiheke Island more. I freakin' love Waiheke. It's only a forty-minute ferry from Auckland's CBD, is warmer than the other regions and is home to wineries with stunning ocean views. Keep an eye out for their

[12] Based off the TKM's directory of Māori iwi (tribes) and organisations.

ballsy yet sophisticated Syrah and weighty Pinot Gris. Make sure you hire a car or bike though. (I made the mistake of walking and could only see three wineries as a result. Though while trekking up and down those hills, I met my friend Nneka, who had made the same mistake as me. So it worked out.)

## Hawke's Bay

Māori region: Tākitimu

Known for:

- Syrah
- Chardonnay
- Pinot Noir
- Red blends

With plenty of sunshine and a lovely ol' climate, Hawke's Bay is a winner for refined Syrah, full-bodied Chardonnay, berry-packed Pinot Noir and elegant red blends. If you love *The Great Gatsby*, visit the beautiful town of Napier while you're in the area. After a devastating earthquake in 1931, the town had to be rebuilt completely, thus giving Napier its distinct Art Deco architecture. They also have an Art Deco Festival every year. It is BANANAS. When I went a few years ago I was most definitely the youngest person there, but it was a great excuse to wear a flapper dress and I regret nothing.

WINE REGIONS WE THINK ARE PRETTY GRAPE

141

# SOUTH ISLAND

## Central Otago

Māori region: Waipounamu

Known for:

- Pinot Noir
- Riesling
- Sauvignon Blanc
- Chardonnay

Get flanked by large, snow-capped mountains while you sip on silken Pinot Noir. (Becky gives a particular shout-out to Burn Cottage Vineyard and Rippon Vineyard.) Central Otago also produces aromatic Riesling, crisp Sauvignon Blanc and elegant Chardonnay. It's New Zealand's southernmost wine region and proud of it. Adrenaline junkies should go via Queenstown and get their fix of skydiving, skiing, jet boating or white water rafting. (Just be sure to buy travel insurance first.)

## Marlborough

Māori region: Te Tau Ihu and Waipounamu

Known for:

- Sauvignon Blanc
- Pinot Noir
- Chardonnay

When most people think 'Kiwi wine', they think 'Marlborough'. Located at the northeast tip of the South Island, it's the country's largest wine region and, in the words of winemaker Michael Ng, it's 'a Sauvignon Blanc factory'. Its zippy Sauvy catapulted New Zealand onto the world stage in the 80s. However, Marlbz can also do a beauuutifully refined Pinot Noir and complex Chardonnay, too.

Take advantage of the sunny, dry climate by kayaking in the clear waters of the Marlborough Sounds. If you want to escalate the situation, splurge on a scenic flight, get a bird's eye view of the water and pretend you are Beyoncé for a day.

WINE
REGIONS
WE
THINK
ARE
PRETTY
GRAPE

143

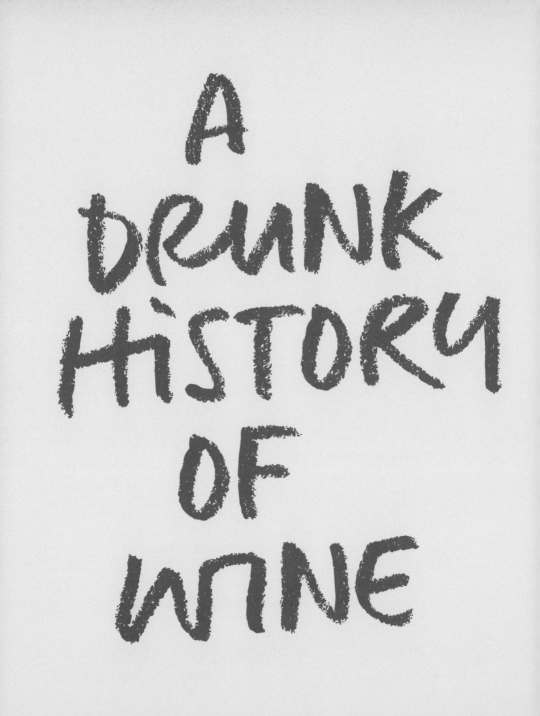

# A DRUNK HISTORY OF WINE

'YOU'VE GOT TO TRY
THIS MEDICINE.
IT'S AMAZING.
SERIOUSLY. PUT IT
IN YOUR MOUTH.'

The Persian concubine who
accidentally discovered
fermented grape juice[1]

[1] No historical sources back up this quote. Not one.

HISTORY WAS ALWAYS one of my favourite subjects throughout high school[1]. But you know what makes it more fun? Alcohol. This chapter draws influence from one of my most beloved TV shows, *Drunk History*, and will tell you the story of wine in a VERY laidback style. The facts remain true, but the telling may be slightly embellished. Think wildly anachronistic dialogue and no scholarly referencing of primary or secondary sources in sight. It's the history of wine made tastier. Feel free to whip out one of these stories at a dinner party or on a first date. I won't tell 'em who hooked you up.

## Super happy fun task for winos

Before we start, what do you already know about wine's history? List all the countries you know that have a history of winemaking.

_____

_____

_____

_____

_____

_____

---

[1] Shoutout to Ms Wobith!

Alright, so where to begin? The earliest winemakers were probably cave peeps who picked and stored wild grapes, then let the leftover grape juice ferment in a dent in a rock (or another makeshift container). Let's call that 'rock wine'. Rock wine was a happy accident that kind of sucked, but had mad potential. Over ensuing millennia people experimented with different techniques. You know, like whether to let vines grow up trees or train them onto trellises[2]; whether certain types of soil suited certain vines better; whether the ferment should go in animal skins, amphorae[3], barrels or tanks; whether to add preservatives; whether to leave wine on lees[4]; how to blend different grape varieties. A lot of factors were (and continue to be) in play. Trial and error has always been key.

As time went on wine was used in religious ceremonies, for medicinal purposes and as an opportunity for people to get loosey-goosey with each other. Perceptions of wine have oscillated wildly. It has been praised as the nectar of the gods, but also derided as a destructive handmaiden for Beelzebub himself. It has been seen as both a sign of civility and a threat to society. Meanwhile, attitudes towards drunkenness have ranged from quaint and amusing to shame-inducing, family-ruining and downright immoral (depending on class, gender and historical context).

[2] **TRELLIS** = the wires and posts that hold up the vines and keep 'em upright.

[3] **AMPHORA** = a Greek or Roman jar with handles, used to store yummy foodstuffs like olive oil and wine. Amphorae is the plural.

[4] **LEES** = dead yeast cells that can add a creamy texture to the palate.

# IRAN, GEORGIA & ARMENIA

Let's start from the very beginning (a very good place to start). The history of winemaking kicks off in the East. From as early as 8500BC, bits of earthenware jars, grape stalks and tartaric acid[5] suggest that wine production first took place in parts of western and northern Iran, Georgia and Armenia. The first cultivated (not wild and free) grape seeds have been found in Georgia, and they date all the way back to 6000BC. (They be old!)

When it comes to origin stories about wine, historian Rod Phillips[6] tells a classic tale about Persian King Jamsheed. To grossly paraphrase, King Jamsheed – who was really into grapes – stored a bunch in jars, forgot about them, then got super pissy when he realised his grapes had gone sour and bubbly. Apparently he labeled the jars as poisonous and went back to his busy schedule of playing Nintendo 64 or whatever. Meanwhile, a lady from his royal harem had a bad headache and was like, 'Nah, I'm over this. Going to top myself.' She then finds the jars marked 'POISON – NO TOUCHIES' and guzzles as many as she can. Instead of dying, she falls asleep and when she wakes her headache is gone[7]. She then goes to the king and says, 'You have got to try this medicine. It's amazing. Seriously. Put it in your mouth.' And he does and thinks, *Mmm, medicinal.* Iran then goes on to make more wine.

While Iran eventually stops making wine after coming under Islamic rule, Georgia can't quit wine – much like Jake can't quit

[5] **TARTARIC ACID** = the most common form of acid in grapes and wine. (Malic acid is the other principal acid found in grapes.)

[6] Author of *A Short History of Wine*. I've gleaned many of my stories from him.

[7] This is the exact opposite reaction I've had to wine benders.

Heath in *Brokeback Mountain*. To this day, Georgia has a super interesting offering of indigenous varieties, like Goruli Mtsvane and Rkatsiteli. Despite political turbulence with Russia, Russia is still the largest importer of Georgian wine.

Armenia? It's not a wine power player anymore, but table wine is still a thing there. Armenia was occupied by the sherry-loving Soviets from the 1930s-90s, slowing down production of other wine styles. The soil in the valleys of the South Caucasus is super lush and some sweet, sweet reds come from there. Ask for Areni or Khndoghni if you're looking for native Armenian reds.

# EGYPT & TURKEY

Egyptian tombs, tablets and some saucy banquet scenes point to how in 3100BC, pharaohs were all the rage and fermented bevvies made from red grapes were used in religious ceremonies. This has a lot to do with wine's resemblance to blood and its mood-altering qualities. Wine was for the social elite, while beer was for the masses. It was used in religious rituals as an offering to the gods and stored in tombs for thirsty pharaohs in the afterlife. When they cracked open his tomb in 1922, the boy-king Tutankhamen had three dozen jars of the good stuff in reserve, and the goddess Hathor even had her own annual wine fest.

Egyptian banquet scenes don't shy away from showing the less-than-flattering sides of excessive drinking – many feature men and women barfing while others get freaky on the floor. My fave quote comes from a tomb that depicts a woman saying, 'Give me eighteen cups of wine. Don't you see I want to get drunk?! My insides are as dry as straw!' (Sounds like someone had a crazy week at the office, amirite?)

Wine was also used for its 'curative properties', prescribed to treat everything from asthma to worms, as a laxative and as a salve on battle wounds. Around the same time, ancient Jews and Phoenicians start to cultivate and spread the gospel of wine. From 1200BC, Phoenicians also trade wine, spreading the joy of plonk across the Mediterranean to the Middle East, Greece and Italy.

Meanwhile, Jews increasingly incorporate wine into their religious ceremonies.

In the book of Genesis we hear how after the flood Noah becomes the first viticulturist and winemaker. As soon as he gets off the Ark, he's like, 'This would make an awesome vineyard, amirite?!' and he plants vines on Mount Ararat (the Taurus Mountains in modern-day eastern Turkey). The story goes that Noah then gets off-his-chops drunk, passes out and inadvertently shows his wiener to his sons.

Wine then crosses from the Jewish to Christian tradition. In the rest of the Bible, the vine gets mentioned more times than any other plant, and symbolises a promised gift from God. When Jesus rocks up, he becomes notorious for being a miracle worker and parable-lover. He gets known for turning water into wine at a wedding feast in Cana and employing wine as a symbol for his own blood. (It's not all lit wedding feasts and symbolism though, there are still many Old and New Testament passages that reference the downside of getting boozed up.)

# GREECE

Around 800BC, the Greeks start to perfect winemaking techniques learned from the Phoenicians. You know, like training vines onto trellises instead of letting them snake up trees. From 300BC, they colonise Egypt and up-skill themselves by abducting Egypt's best horticulturalists and winemakers. Consequently their exported wine grows in demand and the god Dionysus is created in its honour. While men from the Greek upper class drink sweet, full-bodied wine in fancy cups at ritualised events and symposia, the poor consume pale, bitter, low-alcohol wine from ceramic mugs. Even slaves get a wine ration to keep up their strength/calorie intake.

Greece continues to rise in power and soon armies are travelling with stacks of vino. Every time they colonise a new area they plant grapevines. Colonise, plant. Colonise, plant. Some of the earliest colonies include Sicily and southern Italy, before the Greeks travel up the boot to Rome. They also make their mark in wine-less societies like southern France, Germany, Portugal and Spain (though Spain had its own wine thing going, too). Southern Italy was their crowning jewel, though, and they name the region 'Oenotria' or 'the land of trained vines'. Nowadays this area is known for some unique indigenous grapes. Think Assyrtiko from Santorini and Dafni and Kotsifali from Crete.

# ITALY

By 146BC, the Romans have switched up the game and they conquer Greece in the Battle of Corinth. The Roman victors make wine their own, including creating their own wine god, Bacchus, a chubby, wreath-wearing dude who finds a strong female following á la One Direction[8]. Wine becomes an integral part of Roman culture and the Italians further develop the Greeks' cultivation methods. As troops expand across Europe, they plant more vineyards in modern-day France, Germany, Portugal, Spain and Hungary. In the first century BC, they plant vines in Bordeaux and by the early third century, they've planted vines in Burgundy and within a few decades, Alsace. They even have a crack at Britain, but the climate isn't into it, though now, thanks to climate change and rising temperatures, Britain[9] is a late entry in the wine race.

Let the record show that around 100BC, grapes are also being cultivated in India and China (though to a far lesser degree).

Originally, wine was kept for the elite due to its scarcity, but by imperial Rome all social classes are smashing a vino. At that time about 1.8 million hectolitres of wine are being consumed per year. That's about half a litre per day for every man, woman and child in Rome at the time[10]. However, women are looked down upon for drinking, for fear they will get loose and bang

[8]   What can I say, the god knew how to party and he attracted ladies who loved dancing. They were also known as 'maenads'.

[9]   I should mention that England has a long history of importing wine, and that they pioneered using glass bottles for storage in the 1630s. There's also evidence of British vineyards around the 11th century, but French imports ended up being far more popular.

[10]   Though wine was probably not what you'd recognise as wine now. This is because it was often watered down with seawater and flavoured with herbs, spices and sweet, sweet honey. Oh yeah, and boiled in lead-based pots. Nice.

somebody else's husband[11]. You can even legally divorce (or kill) your Roman wife if you find her chug-a-lugging before 194BC[12].

Wine is stored in earthenware amphorae and poured through a sieve before being quaffed. In 79AD, Mount Vesuvius erupts and Pompeii (a super important wine-shipping port) becomes toast. As a result, there's a shortage in wine in Italy, followed by a spike in price. This causes a rush to plant vineyards, which leads to overproduction of wine and in 92AD Emperor Domitian decrees 'Hey! Stop planting vineyards! You're using all the good land up!' The land ban lasts until about 280AD. Meanwhile the Roman contact with the Gauls (now France) influences them to use oak barrels from 200AD. The French are all 'Uh, we've been doing that for ages, copy cats' before skulking off for a cigarette and baguette.

From 200 to 400AD, wine in the Roman Empire kicks goals and advances its practices. This is followed by a period of 1200 to 1400 years during which progress in wine technology slows and is generally restricted to monastic religious orders in Western Europe. That's because in 380AD, Christianity becomes the state religion of the Roman Empire, and wine becomes a crucial part of the sacrament. Inadvertently this helps increase wine's cultural capital. The Catholic Church gets right into wine production throughout the Dark Ages, going so far as to encourage monks to work as winemakers in Italy and France. To this day, wine continues to be part of the Christian Eucharist.

In the late Middle Ages, Italy also gains renown for their smaller region of **Chianti** and its iconic red blend, as well as for pioneering

[11]   This is also a thing in Greece. Guys, just chill.

[12]   Hands up if you would not survive in ancient Rome.

glass wine cups[13] in Venice. Until the 17th century, the most common wine vessels were cups made from silver, pottery, leather or wood. The northwest regions of Barolo and Barbaresco also distinguish themselves during the 19th century for their fragrant Nebbiolo.

Skip ahead to the 1960s when the Denominazione di Origine Controllata (DOC) regulations get created. These regulations (much like the French AoC) aim to ensure quality by defining shizz like regions, grape varieties, maximum yields, levels of alcohol, acidity and extract levels. In 1963, an additional level of certification is added called DOCG (the extra G is for 'e Garantita' to help guarantee top quality).

TRUE OR FALSE **Old World wine is better than New World wine**

What a statement! But no, not necessarily. Old World simply refers to European and Middle Eastern wine regions that are considered the birthplaces of wine, places like Italy, France, Germany, Greece and Israel. New World refers to the rest of the world, the wine regions that sprung up post-15th century. Admittedly, they can vary quite a bit in style, with Old World often being associated with tradition and cooler climates, and New World being aligned with experimentation, technology and warmer climates. But, gun to my head, I'd say the terms indicate history and geography, not quality.

---

[13]   Though England were the ones that went on to make glass wine cups more affordable.

# FRANCE

A LOT happens in France from the Romans onwards, so strap in for
a wild ride. First up, the upshot of being viciously colonised by the
Roman Empire is that France totally nails wine. Post-Roman Empire,
winemaking is encouraged by the land-owning Church and literate
monks who have the science know-how to keep up the winemaking
tradition[14]. Plus, from the late 11th to 13th centuries, the Crusades
means lots of vine-worthy land in Western Europe is given to the
wine-lovin' church. Think: you have our extra land, we fight, you
pray for our souls, we meet you in heaven for a phat rave. The monks
even pioneer clarifying white wine with isinglass (fish-bladder) and
red wine with egg whites.

France then goes on to spearhead some pretty fundamental
things we now associate with wine culture, like the chilling of wine,
systematic geographical naming[15] and varietal labelling. So it makes
sense that France goes on to be one of the biggest and most iconic
wine producers.

Other areas that help to make French wine famous include the
northern region of  Champagne . Champagne benefits from the
emergence of regulated hygiene
measures in the late eighth century.
Plus, during that time, the city of
Reims becomes the go-to place
for coronations. All the way up
until the 17th century, bubbles
in wine are considered a fault by

[14]  So much so that, for a long time, the Cistercian order
in Burgundy didn't have to pay taxes because
their wine was très magnifique.

[15]  Mixing wine from different winemakers was common
in the 17th century and dependent on a merchant's
whim. By the 18th century, more emphasis was put on
grape varieties, and attention paid to which wines were
coming from which estate. This is mostly
due to some clever marketing by the Pontac family
in Bordeaux, who used scarcity as a selling point
for their fine wines.

producers, such as such as Dom Pierre Pérignon. But bubbles soon become a commodity when they are introduced to the English by Marquis de St-Evremond. It's only in the 19th century, in the court of Philippe II, that the French nobility start to dig this fault, too. Actual quote from the time[16], 'Our old king who didn't like bubbles is dead and this new guy seems cool. So let's get our bubble on[17].'

In the late 18th century, Nicole-Barbe Clicquot-Ponsardin (AKA the Widow Clicquot) pioneers riddling[18] and disgorgement[19] with Veuve Clicquot. As we already know, the region of Champagne trademarks its fizz in 1891 (and further protects its name and clever techniques in the 1990s). Eventually, iconic Champagne labels like Cristal and Dom Pérignon get Hollywood-famous as a pricey drop ideal for conspicuous consumption.

From the 13th century onwards, the southwestern region of **Bordeaux** becomes iconic for Cabernet, Merlot, Sauvy and Semillon. The region becomes the main supplier of grog to the English royalty, so much so that it still prospers throughout the late 1340s, while the Black Death wipes out almost a third of Europe's population. Individual producers are called 'châteaux' and ranked into divisions in 1855. To this day, Bordeaux has a rep for some of the most expensive wines in the world, particularly its 'first growths'[20].

To the east, **Burgundy** gets Kardashian-famous for its Pinot

A
DRUNK
HISTORY
OF
WINE

[16] For the record, absolutely NOT a quote from the time.

[17] If you're interested in learning more about the region, *A Year in Champagne* is a solid doco to watch.

[18] **RIDDLING** = rotating inverted wine bottles clockwise and anti-clockwise to help sediment collect at the neck (just in time for disgorgement).

[19] **DISGORGEMENT** = ejecting grapey sediment from sparkling wine to ensure that the wine will be clear.

[20] **FIRST GROWTHS** = also known as Premier cru. The wines and estates that are at the highest level in the Grand cru classification system in France, for example, Château Latour, Château Margaux and Château Haut-Brion.

Noir, Chardonnay, and a steep, limestone slope known as Côte-d'Or[21]. (Though post-Black Death, Burgundy did have a crack at Gamay, however Philip the Bold rips those vines out and replaces them with its trademark Pinot Noir in 1395 because he hated the taste of hardy Gamay so much.) From the Middle Ages (until now), individual producers are referred to as 'domaines' and are ranked and delineated by appellation[22] (with Grand Crus at the top and Appellations Régionales at the bottom of the pile).

Meanwhile, Beaujolais in east-central France becomes famous for fruity Gamay and Chardonnay. So famous that it gets its own day in November to celebrate the region's Beaujolais Nouveau[23]. Its Internet-fame peaks in 2015 when wine documentary *Somm: Into the Bottle* popularises the region's Crus[24] and how undervalued they are.

(There are also mega advances and historical moments for regions like Alsace on the German border, Côtes du Rhône in the southeast, Jura in the east, Languedoc-Roussillon in the south, Sauvy-loving Loire and Provence in southeast France. There's everything from the French Revolution to Napoleon expanding the French empire like a demon[25]. France pioneers vine-disease control

[21] An escarpment stretching all the way from Dijon to the town of Beaune, known for its vineyards.

[22] **APPELLATION** = a region where certain grapes are grown and particular winemaking regulations are in play. France and Italy have the most famous bunch, for example, Anjou, Chablis, Champagne, Friuli-Venezia Giulia, Piedmont.

[23] **BEAUJOLAIS NOUVEAU** = wine from Beaujolais that is made 6-8 weeks post-harvest (which is why some winos won't go near it. Not aged enough for 'em.)

[24] **CRU** = growth.
**GRAND CRU** = great growth. Kind of a complicated term though as it varies from region to region in whether it's referring to the top vineyards (Burgundy), wineries (Bordeaux) or village it comes from (Champagne).
**BEAUJOLAIS CRU** = wine that comes from one of the region's top ten vineyard sites.

[25] Napoleon's empire even invaded northern Portugal, making its trade with Britain super expensive.

and vine hybridisation in the 1800s, as well as defining wine as being made from grapes or grape juice in 1907. France also set up the Appellation d'Origine Contrôlée (AoC)[26] regulations in 1908. Unfortunately my word count is limited so history buffs should overcome these knowledge gaps by Googling each region while you drink.

Ooh, but I have to tell you about phylloxera epidemic[27] in the 1860s. These tiny yellow aphids (AKA assholes) completely devastate France and – by default – most of the winemaking world[28]. There are no quarantine restrictions between the US and France from 1858 to 1862 and the US export their vines to Europe, and consequently our itty bitty mates, phylloxera. While vines indigenous to North America can tolerate these little dudes, the more dainty Vitis Vinifera[29] don't fare so well. It is not a fun time for Europe and the end result is they have to import LOADS of wine. They also have to rip up their vines and replant with disease-resistant American rootstock, which the French were pretty mad about at first. But these new grafted French vines with Americano roots do so well that by the 1980s many regions have to do vine-pull schemes to combat over-production.

[26] **APPELLATION D'ORIGINE CONTRÔLÉE (AOC)** = much like Italy's DOC, it guarantees the product comes from a certain French region and holds up certain standards.

[27] **PHYLLOXERA** = the yellow aphids that made Europe (and the rest of the winemaking world) its bish in the 1860s.

[28] This actually really sucks because it knocked out wine industries that couldn't afford to replant, like Peru in the 1970s.

[29] **VITIS VINIFERA** = traditionally European vine varieties.

# GERMANY

All right, let's backtrack a little (like in one of those TV series with parallel timelines à la *Westworld*). Back in 6AD, the Romans bust in. They plant vineyards in Deutschland and kick off their industry. But then Germanic tribes invade them right back throughout the third and fifth centuries, marking the fall of the Roman Empire. The wine-snob Romans think the Germans are barbarians for drinking undiluted vino and for loving beer. The Germans also get a rep for being rubbish at viticulture as there's a downtick in wine production. (Though this is more likely due to the effects of political instability across the empire rather than schlocky maintenance.) Basically, beer is all the rage in Germany during this time.

Yet by the early Christian period[30] a couple of centuries later, tables be turned. Beer is out and wine is in. Drinking wine is seen as a symbol of conversion. By the 11th and 12th centuries, more and more land is dedicated to viticulture, particularly around the Rhine, Main and Mosel rivers, but after a series of wars and bad harvests, many Germans return to beer in the late 17th century. However, wine comes back into fashion in the 1800s and they have to import French and Italian vino to keep up with domestic demand. It's also around this time that Europeans stop adding lead to wine as a sweetener and bacteria fighter. (Yes, that was a thing. No, it was not – and still isn't – good for you.)

In the 20th century, Deutschland is hugely affected by World War One and loses the delish Rieslings and Gewürtztraminers of Alsace to France. Plus, the Treaty of Versailles forces Germany to import French wine free of tariffs,

---

30   Pre-First Council of Nicaea in 325AD.

which massively undercuts their local production. From the 1970s onwards, Germany becomes increasingly synonymous with the Riesling varietal, most notably in the Mosel Valley where it's at its most delicate and light in alcohol. Southern regions like the Rhine and Pfalz rack up a reputation for producing wines (like the dark-skinned Dornfelder varietal) that are a bit heavier, while wines with 'Auslese' on the label[31] are known for being sweet.

# ALGERIA

You may not associate Algeria with wine, but French colonisation made sure they had vino (and ensured they played a huge role in supplying France with wine during the Great French Wine Blight[32] in the mid-19th century). Before the French arrive in the 19th century, the Phoenicians plant vineyards around 1250BC. But Islamic rule soon puts a dampener on that idea – they rip up a tonne of vineyards in the 7th century.

When France bowls into Algeria in 1830, they start replanting vineyards. When the French wine industry gets decimated by phylloxera in the 1860-70s, wine production in Algeria soars. They export the shizz out of Algerian wine, particularly in the 1930s. However, when the French cede control of the country in 1962, wine production goes into decline. So if you're hoping to find an Algerian vino at your bottle-o, make sure to pack your time machine too.

A DRUNK HISTORY OF WINE

31  Another thing you might find on a German label is the term 'Qualitatswein'. It's a quality classification that 95% of German wines meet.

32  That is, when the yellow aphids made vines their bish.

# PORTUGAL & SPAIN

Let's circle back to mainland Europe. Let's zero in on Portugal and Spain. Post-Roman colonisation and the rise of Islam slows the progress of viticulture in Portugal and Spain. The Spanish get around certain laws by insisting wine made from dates is fine, but in the 10th century the caliph Osman is like, 'Uh Valencia, I'm not buying it. You need to get rid of two-thirds of your vineyards.' But the region's vineyards soon bounce back in the 12th century when Christian rule returns.

In the 1500s, the Spanish wine industry makes huge leaps forward and its sweeter, more alcoholic wine becomes popular both locally and in merry old England (thanks to England's beef with France). Sherry from Jerez (then known as 'sack') even gets a name drop by Shakespeare in *Henry IV*. Spain's wine trade is also helped by its political stability. Unlike the rest of northern Europe at the time, Spain avoids the political volatility brought on by the Protestant Reformation.

From the 1520s to 60s, Spanish missionaries spread wine to the Americas, including Mexico, Peru, Chile, Argentina and California. They plant so much over this forty-year period that the Spanish government eventually freaks out and tries to put restrictions on their flourishing wine industry. Safe to say, the restrictions fail miserably and Chile and Argentina continue to kick wine goals to this day[33].

## FAST FACT
Catholics and Protestants both use wine in their rituals, though some evangelical Protestants supported temperance movements in the 19th century.

---

[33] Peru was also a contender for a while, but had a huge phylloxera epidemic in the late 19th century that they never recovered from.

Meanwhile, in 1543 the Portuguese sail to Japan, bringing the feudal lords some vino as a gift from Saint Francis Xavier. Jesuit priests convert a whole bunch of Japanese people to Catholicism and the joys of wine. But by 1587, the party's over and vino-loving Christianity is banned from Japan. Wine consumption drops accordingly.

Portugal has a big moment in 1679 when the English parliament bans French wines (the ban is then reversed in 1697). Porto (or 'port wine', wine fortified by brandy) was all the rage, especially from the UNESCO World Heritage site of the Douro Valley . Demand exceeds supply, though, and they start creating weird blends with lesser vintages then adding sugar and spices like ginger, cinnamon and pepper, which leads to regulation by the Portuguese government. When English demand lessens, the Portuguese export heavily to their West African colonies throughout the 1860s. Over twenty-three million litres of distilled wine is exported. Portugal also gets famous for being one of the largest producers of cork[34].

By the 2000s, Portugal becomes better known for planting distinctive grape varieties – Tempranillo, Touriga Franca, Touriga Nacional and Baga to name a few. Unfortunately, around the same time, the cork industry goes to poop when premium winemakers start to blame cork for tainting their wines with a dank, mouldy taste. As a result, Australia pioneers the Stelvin – screw caps. Cork sales fall, but eventually Portugal cleans up its act and buy some robots with incredible sensors and X-rays to detect TCA[35] contamination better.

[34]   Spain also is a big cork producer from the 1600s onwards. They even set up the first major cork production facility in the 1750s.

[35]   **TCA** = the compound largely responsible for cork taint.

# CHILE & ARGENTINA

South America has a growing wine industry that's worth getting to know[36]. It all begins with Spanish missionaries coming to Chile in the 1550s. They establish Chile's first winery. Only a few years later, in 1556, they travel from Chile to Argentina and plant grapes in the Mendoza region. Eventually Chile gets recognised for its ability to avoid common vine diseases, thanks to its relative isolation. Its plantings of Cabernet Sauvignon, Merlot, Chardonnay and Sauvy do super well.

In Argentina, vineyards at the foothills of the Andes flourish and certain producers start to note specific elevations on their labels (usually above 1,000 metres, which European wineries find strange since they usually only don't go over 500 metres max). Cabernet Sauvignon and Chardonnay do quite well in the land of tango, however, it's velvety Malbec that eventually becomes synonymous with Argentine wine.

# THE UNITED STATES OF AMERICA

The first all-American wine is made in 1680 by French Huguenots in Florida. They had made attempts with European grapes before, but this is the first successful attempt with indigenous grapes. Plot twist: the Huguenots actually spend more time making wine than setting up camp and Englishman John Hawkins

[36] I recently discovered Uruguay's national grape Tannat and I'm all about this earthy, Shiraz-like varietal now.

has to bail them out with food and supplies. A direct quote: 'You guys are idiots and this wine is rubbish.'[37]

## Not so pure(itan)

The Puritans get a bad rap for slowing down the progress of wine in America, but they actually drank wine (in moderation) in the 17th century. It's not until the 19th century that they get caught up in the anti-alcohol movement.

Spanish missionary Junípero Serra hits town in 1769, spreading Jesus (and vino) to the New World. He makes his way from Mexico City to California with grapes in tow, and opens a mission in San Diego. Spanish missions spread across California, and Franciscan monks don't forget to take their winemaking tradition with them. Sonoma's first winery is established in 1805. The county eventually becomes known for its Chardonnay, Cabernet Sauvignon and Pinot Noir.

In 1785, Thomas Jefferson is appointed the US minister to France. He gets into French wine (espesh Bordeaux and Burgundy). He then returns to the States with a bunch of French grape cuttings. It does not work out. The European vines can't cope with the American climate and the Americans go back to experimenting with indigenous vines.

Meanwhile, one of the signers of the Declaration of Independence, Dr Benjamin Rush, gains popularity as an anti-alcohol advocate. He equates alcohol addiction with crime > financial disaster > immorality > family breakdown.

[37] Not a direct quote.

He sets the foundations for later temperance movements, and eventually Prohibition.

When California has a gold rush in the late 1840s, demand for vino increases and winemaking spreads further across the West Coast. The gold rushers bring vines from the East Coast, including Zinfandel, a varietal from Croatia for which California would become known. By 1880, Cali had produced ten million gallons of wine. By 1905, it was thirty-one million gallons per year. By 1910, they were producing forty-five million gallons of wine.

But by 1920, temperance gives way to Prohibition and anti-alcohol laws are a thing across the whole country. Basically, all intoxicating liquors are banned from being made, transported or sold. Though there are exceptions made for wine used for religious ceremonies, food flavouring and medicinal purposes. (Interesting how demand for sacramental and medicinal wine also spikes dramatically during this period.)

Although Prohibition is finally repealed in 1933, beer actually becomes more popular during the Great Depression because it's cheaper than wine. Plus, class comes into play. Mechanisation leads to a rise in production, and leads to a major shift in culture around the relationship between work and alcohol. While execs can still have boozy business lunches, workers on the assembly line are discouraged from day-drinking, further enforcing stereotypes around wine as an upper-class luxury.

After World War Two, wine production falls into the hands of large companies in places like California (and Oz). In Cali, the big dog is Gallo[38]. Napa, Sonoma and South of the Bay becomes known for Cabernet Sauvignon, Zinfandel,

[38]   In NZ, Corbans and Montana were the big dogs. While in Oz, the industry becomes dominated by Penfolds, Lindeman's and Hardy.

Pinot Noir, Merlot, Chardonnay, Sauvy B and Pinot Gris.

As a result, this trend sets up two sectors in the industry –
bulk winemakers versus premium winemakers. Naturally, captains
of industry like Gallo don't love this distinction as it implies
their wine isn't great. So they spend their monies buying out
smaller producers with quality reps, as well as spending a LOT
on advertising to convince consumers that all Cali wine is bueno.
It's the first time in history that advertising plays such a key role in
the industry. As a result, Californian wines dominate the wine market
throughout the 1960s.

In 1976, American wine hits the world stage when it competes
with France in the one-off event The Paris Tasting. They do a blind

tasting and pit a Cali Cabernet Sauvignon against a red Bordeaux, as well as Cali Chardonnay against white Burgundies. Cali wins. Much shock. Very controversy.

In ensuing decades, even though Cali remains the largest producer in the US by a LONG shot, other regions come to the fore, too. Washington gets cred for bright Cabernet Sauvignon, Merlot, Syrah, Chardy and Riesling. Meanwhile, cool, grey Oregon makes a name for itself, particularly in the Willamette Valley, thanks to its Pinot Noir, Pinot Gris and, more recently, its Chardonnay, which is made from Burgundy clones.

# CANADA

Maybe you don't think of Canada when you think of wine, but they got some history there. To generalise wildly, anyone who speaks French is going to live near wine. Even before the French arrive, Norse explorer Leif Erikson cultivates wild grapes in Canada around 1001AD. But winemaking really kicks off when the French claim Canada as their own in 1534 and Quebec City is firmly established in 1608. Jesuits swoop in and attempt to grow European grapes. The results are not crash hot, so they turn back to the indigenous grapes instead.

Flash forward to now and Canada's two major wine-producing regions are Ontario (particularly Niagara, right near the big-ass falls) and British Columbia . Ontario is famous for Icewine (sweet wine made of frozen grapes) as well as Chardonnay, sparkling wine and some Cabernets.

# SOUTH AFRICA

South Africa is a now considered to be a fairly iconic producer.
But it hasn't always been. First up, the Dutch East India Company
invades South Africa and the sailors are unimpressed that they don't
have wine for their journey back from Africa to Europe. In 1655,
the first governor of the Cape, Jan van Riebeek, plants South
Africa's first vineyard. Unfortunately for old mate Jan, the Dutch
don't have a strong winemaking tradition (brandy was more up
their alley). Despite encouraging farmers to plant more vineyards,
peeps are like, 'Nah, this isn't working, van Rie-geek.' It's only
when the French Huguenots bust into the Cape between 1680 and
1690 that the wine industry really kicks off. The Huguenots allow
longer wait times for the grapes to mature and they practice better
cleanliness during the winemaking process. So by 1752, there are
3.9 million vines in production. (Sorry 'bout it, Jan.)

For centuries, vineyard workers are partially paid in alcohol.
(Yeah, not even exaggerating.) This is known as the 'dop system'
and has deeply, DEEPLY insidious health and social consequences.
So while South Africa's wine industry experiences huge growth
post-18th century, the local population gets screwed over. From
1962, international trade sanctions come into play and affect the wine
industry during their apartheid governments.

A lot of important history happens (that you probz shouldn't
seek to learn from this professional drunk/dance floor ruiner[39]).
Smash-cut to now, when wine
regions are booming in the

[39]    Instead look to anti-apartheid activists like
Nelson Mandela or Steve Biko.

Western Cape near the coast. Currently, the most notable wine district is arguably Franschhoek , known as the 'culinary capital' of the Cape. Then again, the Stellenbosch region holds the most vineyard plantings, so you make up your own mind. Expect reds like Cabernet Sauvignon, Shiraz/Syrah and the uniquely South African clone Pinotage[40]. In the white wine department, keep an eye out for Chenin Blanc, Colombard, Sauvignon Blanc and Chardonnay.

# AUSTRALIA

The First Fleet invades Australia in 1788. Onboard they bring a ton of grape cuttings from South Africa. In 1795, Peter Schaffer is credited as producing the first Aussie wine, but it's no bueno. Newbie winemakers treat Australia like a mini-England, even going so far as to prune vines in January and February – that is, the UK's winter, but our summer[41]. It's not until 1825 that Scottish amateur viticulturist James Busby rolls into Sydney, convinced our wine could be a killer export. This moment is later credited as kicking off Australia's wine industry.

By the 1830s, vineyards are popping up in the Hunter Valley. Dr Christopher Penfold arrives in South Australia in the 1840s and sets up a medical practice on his estate, known as 'The Grange'. Thanks to wine being rich in iron, he offers it to immigrants by prescription to treat their anemia post-journey from Europe to Oz. Meanwhile, Lutherans from Silesia make their mark north of Adelaide in the Barossa Valley .

[40] **PINOTAGE** = a cross between Pinot Noir and Hermitage, created by Professor Abraham Perold in 1925.

[41] Vines are meant to be trimmed in winter, yo.

# WINE AS MEDICINE

**BEN**  My parents have read enough tabloid Chinese media to know that red wine is good for you. I grew up watching my parents drink Guinness, not because they liked it but because Guinness is considered a tonic for Chinese people. So Guinness, especially lukewarm Guinness, isn't drunk out of any semblance of joy, but because it fortifies your blood. Similar to eating red meat for iron, or something like that. (I don't know about the science behind this, by the way.) But they do know that red wine is scientifically proven, in moderation, to be good for you, so they like the idea of it. My mum loves a good drop of red and my dad's getting into it. But he's less discerning about what he does and doesn't like. If it's red and in a glass, he'll drink it for health reasons. It's weird. It's like, 'Dad, it's not vitamins.'

A
DRUNK
HISTORY
OF
WINE

By 1850, Swiss immigrants help establish vineyards near Melbourne and around the  Yarra Valley . Western Australia jumps on the wino bandwagon, too. And it doesn't take long before Aussies are showing off their wares in the UK, France and beyond (though French judges at the 1873 Vienna Exhibition get pretty uppity when they do some blind-tasting and discover their fave wine is from Victoria). At this stage, New World wine is still aiming to mimic Old World varieties. It would be another century before New World styles are accepted on their own terms.

The term 'plonk' gets invented by our soldiers during World

War One. It's basically a bastardisation of the French term 'vin blanc' (low quality wine). This fact makes me weirdly proud to be Australian. Fast-forward to the late 1980s when we dominate the global market and get cred as wine-research-and-development nerds. Unfortunately our worldwide saturation gives us a reputation for mass-produced wines, in particular brassy Chardonnay and highly alcoholic Shiraz. We also get a rep for having one of the highest per-capita rates of wine consumption in the English-speaking world. (Whoops.)

Eventually our fine wine producers get the recognition they deserve, particularly for revolutionary techniques like our canopy management[42] and night harvesting[43]. Our wine prodigies travel to the Northern hemisphere as highly skilled seasonal workers during Oz's off season[44], while Frenchies and the like visit us in their off season. The range of wine knowledge keeps expanding around the world, thanks to globalisation.

At the moment, our tax breaks still favour larger outfits. YET the natural wine movement, particularly in the Adelaide Hills, has brought in a new generation of drinkers. People (like you!) read books like this and drink local, keeping our Aussie vino dream live.

---

[42] **CANOPY MANAGEMENT** = involves using a bunch of vineyard techniques to manage a grapevine's leaves, shoots and fruit. Done throughout winter, pruning all the way until harvest.

[43] **NIGHT HARVESTING** = harvesting grapes at night in order to keep the fruit cool and maintain better control over the fermentation process.

[44] I'm not 100% sure when this is. I imagine post-harvest?

# NEW ZEALAND

Now down to the most southern wine region, New Zealand. In 1832, wino James Busby moves from Oz to New Zealand. He brings with him grape cuttings from Australia and kicks off New Zealand's first vineyard in 1836. Wineries are first established in Auckland, but eventually move down to Marlborough then south again to Central Otago (AKA the world's most southerly region).

By the 1970s, the Kiwis have got this gig sorted and start flogging crisp Sauvignon Blanc like it's going out of style. The success of Sauvy B in this area is partly because of the influence of wine-loving immigrants from Dalmatia (now part of Croatia and Montenegro). Marlborough, in particular, gets known for being a Sauvy factory and to this day their Sauvignon Blancs are Australia's most imported white. NZ also becomes world-famous for fruity and easy-drinking Pinot Noir.

# CHINA

I quite possibly should have popped China at the beginning of this list, not the end, because there's evidence that a fermented wild grape juice with rice and honey was being consumed in China in 7000BC. However, it wasn't until the 1980s that China began importing French wine under Deng Xiaoping.

But what's exciting about the wine industry in China now is how forward-thinking it is. A lot of money and Old World expertise is being poured into their burgeoning wine industry and savvy commercial wineries are increasingly marketing their goods to the growing middle and upper classes. International wine awards have been won and many Cabernet blends have been kicking goals for years.

China self-report that they have seven growing regions, plus 40+ indigenous grape varieties that are exclusive to them. It's rumoured that there are over 12,000 acres of Grenache vineyards in existence. So while China doesn't have an iconic winemaking tradition quite yet, it's definitely one to watch.

SO THERE YOU HAVE IT, a pocket-sized history of wine to give you some context for your favourite drank. It's safe to say that there is a whole world (and history) of wine outside France and Italy. What will you try next?

## Super happy fun task for winos

Now, you're across wine history and ready to write a (fairly short and campy) thesis about it, list all the countries you didn't realise had a history of winemaking and/or stories you want to remember.

_____

_____

_____

_____

_____

# TIME OUT

Having a month off alcohol can be a great way to give your liver a rest and help raise money for a great cause. You can do this on your own or join a not-for-profit challenge. Here in Australia, there's FebFast (supporting at-risk young people), Dry July (raising funds for cancer support organisations) and OcSober (fundraising for Life Education Australia).

Taking a month off alcohol is also a helpful way to check in on your drinking. If you're struggling to have two to three alcohol-free days a week, you've noticed that hangovers or your drunk self are affecting your work and/or personal relationships, or you find it hard to unwind without a vino, it might be a good time to:

- Have a chat with your GP
- Check out HelloSundayMorning.org
- Google 'Alcohol and Drug Foundation' or call 1300 85 85 84.

A
DRUNK
HISTORY
OF
WINE

175

'MAYBE I JUST
DON'T KNOW WHAT
I'M MISSING. MAYBE
I THINK ALL WINE
TASTES THE SAME
BECAUSE I'M DRINKING
ALL SHIT WINE.'

Rosie Waterland

**WELL, YOU'VE MADE IT** to the end of this book in one piece. And look at you – all full of wine knowledge and what not! It's kinda impressive to think that one little beverage could be so intertwined with politics and wars, shape social and economic change, mark shifts in diet and taste, play an integral role in religious rituals and medicine AND be damn delicious, isn't it?

'But wait, wait,' you say. 'We've only just scratched the surface of this whole wine palaver and I have the equivalent of intellectual blue balls RN.'

Well, first up – that's a bit graphic, reader.

Secondly, I'm glad you're still interested in this leviathan-sized topic. There is just SO much vino to try and explore. Give yourself permission to ask questions and really enjoy this journey. Keep reading, watching and tasting your way to better wine knowledge. Here are a few resources I found particularly helpful and/or entertaining AF.

STILL CURIOUS?

179

# READ

- *The 24-Hour Wine Expert* by Jancis Robinson
  A top British wine expert gives you 112 pages of
  snackable wine info – stuff like common wine myths,
  matching wine with food as well as more info on
  regions. She's rad.
- *A Short History of Wine* by Rod Phillips
  For the history nerds, this is a more in-depth
  understanding of wine throughout history by a Kiwi
  wine writer/historian/judge based in Canada.
- *Wine. All the Time.* by Marissa A. Ross
  Super approachable book about wine from an
  American writer and humourist. Love the practical
  'Regions to Recognise' segment, as well as the sound
  advice offered in 'How to drink with your boss and not
  lose your job'.
- *Wine Folly* by Madeline Puckette & Justin Hammack
  Uber-practical American wine toolkit with illustrations
  to boot.
- *Wine Grapes: A Complete Guide to 1,368 Vine
  Varieties Including Their Origins and Flavours* by Jancis
  Robinson, José Vouillamoz & Julia Harding
  A thorough dissection of all the known grape varietals
  by IRL wine experts.

# NETFLIX & SWILL

- *Chateau Chunder: A Wine Revolution*
  A funny doco (with fantastically camp re-enactments)
  about the history of Aussie wine, in particular how its
  global reputation has evolved over the last sixty years.
  Includes cameos from wine writers Huon Hooke, Oz
  Clarke, Jancis Robinson and James Halliday.
- *Decanted*
  A doco about the 2015 vintage in the Napa Valley,
  California. Good insight into the wine-growing process,
  American wine history, and what the heck vine clones are.
  Ten points to Heidi Barrett for flying herself to work in a
  helicopter and selling a half-million-dollar bottle of vino.
- *Drunk History* (BOTH the British and American versions)
  Yeah, you're not going to bump up your wine
  knowledge here, but it's a very fun show. Basically, a
  comedian/writer gets liquored up and retells their
  favourite story from history. It then gets re-enacted
  by actors in historical get-up, using the storyteller's
  exact (often garbled) dialogue.  My most beloved ep
  is season one, ep four of the American version when
  Jen Kirkman tells the story of Puritan maverick Mary
  Dyer after a few vinos. My MVPs are Winona Ryder
  and Michael Cera for their ability to bring to life Jen's
  inebriated narration.

STILL
curious?

181

- *The Family Law*

  Like Ben? Then you'll love his show, *The Family Law*. Take a break from the 50 Shades of White[1] that is Australian television and get ready to LOL.
- *The Flying Winemaker*

  If you're interested in the Asian wine market and more adventurous wine choices, this is a great doco series to dog-ear on Netflix. Follow Eddie McDougall (winemaker and owner of the Hong Kong wine shop, The Flying Winemaker) as he wines his way around Hong Kong, Thailand, Bali, Japan, India, Taiwan, and Australia. This show has added heaps of items to my bucket list, including:
  - Go to the Hong Kong Wine & Dine festival
  - Taste vino in Nashik Valley, India
  - Sample Chinese wines in a Scottish castle at Treaty Port Vineyards
  - Try a Grace Vineyard sparkling in China
  - Have a crack at Japan's indigenous Koshu grape from Château Mercian
  - Do a wine tour at Grover Zampa in Bengaluru

[1]   That phrase is copyright of Ben Law. The man is a one-stop quote shop and if I had it my way this book would just be a transcript of my wines with him.

- *The Katering Show*
  HOOH MAMA, I flippin' love this web series (and their follow-up show, *Get Krackin'*). In *The Katering Show*, Kate McCartney and Kate McLennan pair up as a food intolerant and an intolerable foodie. Winos, treat yourself to 'The Booze Revooze'. (You. Are. Welcome.)
- *Key & Peele* (Season Four, Episode Four)
  Keegan-Michael Key talking about wine-tasting and using descriptors like 'ashtray' is bueno.
- *The Real Housewives of Auckland*
  I took Ben's advice and binge-watched this over two days (because I'm an effin' winner who lives a fast-paced life). You will learn little to nothing about Champagne, but the show is outrageous. Come for Anne the Champagne (and Cat) Lady, stay for Gilda's beautiful bluntness. The friendships in this show have some real moments of loveliness, but – trigger warning – the fights have drawn the attention of the Human Rights Commission. (I do not jest. Some racist shit goes down.) Best enjoyed with a few bottles of sparkling (or Champagne for those with the Benjamins).
- *Red Obsession*
  Aussie doco narrated by Russell Crowe about the rise in popularity of Bordeaux's Premier cru[2] as a form of conspicuous consumption in China. One to watch for those interested in China's growing love of wine.

STILL CURIOUS?

183

[2] **PREMIER CRU** = also known as 'First Growth'. The wines and estates that are at the highest level in the Grand cru classification system in France, for example, Château Latour, Château Margaux and Château Haut-Brion.

- *Sideways*

  Okay, so no doubt you've heard about this movie, but I'd be remiss not to mention it. It's a darkly funny film, with some comic but difficult characters, that totally romanticises winemaking. But come on, the world is burning and we could all use some romance RN.

- *Somm*

  An American doco following four sommeliers aiming to pass the crazy-difficult Master Sommelier exam. Warning: if you're the competitive type, it might make you want to upend your life and become a Master Somm.

- *Somm: Into the Bottle*

  All the off-cuts of Somm, plus extra follow-up interviews with the sommeliers. Brian McClintic manages to get freakin' fit between the two docos and it's worth seeing the film for that transformation alone.

- *Sour Grapes*

  If you like crime docos, this is for you. The story of a brilliant wine counterfeiter/pathological liar/wine lover.

- *The Truth About Alcohol*

  British doco where dreamy emergency doctor Javid Abdelmoneim investigates the science of drinking, including why red wine is considered better for you than white, how alcohol affects sleep and what the best hangover cures are.

# LISTEN

- *Everything Happens For A Riesling*
  **IT ME!** This is my new podcast where I have a wine
  with wine. I've rounded up a bunch of my comedian
  and writer friends and got them to embody their
  favourite wine varietal for fifteen minutes as we share
  a glass together and I ask loaded questions.
- *My Dad Wrote A Porno*
  A podcast comprised of Jamie Morton reading out his
  dad's erotic novel, *Belinda Blinked*, much to the disgust
  and chagrin of his witty mates, Alice Levine and James
  Cooper. The protagonist, Belinda, seems to subsist
  entirely on a diet of chilled Chilean and Australian
  Chardonnay. A true work of genius by the irreplaceable
  Rocky Flintstone. Five stars.
- *The Philosopher's Zone* ('Wine: A Matter of Taste' ep)
  Radio National at its most moreish. This ep features
  Professor Barry Smith from the University of London
  talking about the philosophy of wine, in particular the
  differences between expert and novice wine drinkers
  (spoiler alert: novices don't realise they can taste just
  as well). They also cover the subjectivity/objectivity of
  taste, flavour versus flavour perception, the problem
  with wine writing and the difference between individual
  preference and judging quality. Plus, he runs through
  a tasting in a really practical, step-by-step way. Highly
  recommend this bad boy.

STILL
CURIOUS?

- *The Unbearable Lightness of Being Hungry*
  Super foodie Lee Tran Lam talks to food and wine professionals about their career highlights, war stories and where they love to eat in Sydney. I dig the ep with Ambrose Chiang, Head Sommelier at Momofuku Seiobo, for his story about mixing up very exxy and cheap wine, as well as their chat about the differences in Eastern and Western dining culture.

# INSTA-STALK

Oh gosh, there are so many quality wine-related accounts to creep on. Here are my top six.

- @caitlyn_rees
  Head somm at Fred's Sydney. She travels a lot. She has a nice fringe. She posts aspirational wines.
- @citywineshop
  Wine inspo from this popular Melbourne CBD bottle shop and wine bar.
- @cultofthevine
  Another rad source of wine inspo. Self-proclaimed natural wine store and bar that delivers Australia wide.
- @ericwareheim
  The very tall dude from *Master of None*, who also owns the Californian wine label Las Jaras Wines. Posts cat vids sometimes, too.
- @thedogsofwine
  Need I say more?
- @winerepublic
  A Melbourne independent retailer and online store that does super-stylised shots of their products. It's the goods.

And you can follow me @wineinaonesie if you want to stay in touch.

# GLOSSARY

A CHEAT SHEET of common, but often confusing, wine terms. So I don't overwhelm you with a giant list, I've broken this section up into sections – Wine 101, Old World-y, and Technical/Sciencey terms. Knowledge is power, fam.

# WINE 101 TERMS

**Acid:** the acidity from the grapes and fermentation process. Keeps the wine bright and refreshing, as well as ensuring bacteria knows its place.

**Aeration:** letting a wine breeeeeathe by exposing it to air. Helps to soften the wine's tannins and acidity.

**Age-worthy:** improves in quality and taste through ageing.

**Alcohol:** the fun bit of wine. Without it, you'd have grape juice.

**Amphora:** a Greek or Roman jar with handles, used to store yummy foodstuffs like olive oil and wine. Amphorae is the plural.

**Astringent:** usually in reference to whites. A wine that feels a bit sharp, prone to making your lips pucker.

**Balanced/has nice balance:** when a wine feels pretty bang on. All the components – acid, tannin, alcohol and fruit – are as harmonious as an unlikely animal pairing.

**Blend:** when a couple of different varieties are used to make a wine.

**Body:** how heavy the wine feels in your mouth when you drink it. Typically, light, medium or full-bodied.

**Bordeaux glass:** taller, less bowl-like wine glasses that encourage wine to head to the back of the mouth. Ideal for full-bodied reds.

**Bouquet:** the aromas of a wine. You might also hear about how a wine is 'on the nose'. Same diff, effectively.

**Brassy:** when a wine is harsh and a bit loud.

**Burgundy glass:** rounder, bowl-like wine glasses that better capture the wine's aromas. Perfect for more delicate vinos like Pinot Noir.

GLOSSARY

**Chewy:** textural term for wine that dries out the inside of your mouth, giving it an almost food-like quality. Not necessarily a bad thing!

191

**Creamy:** textural term usually used in reference to white or sparkling wines. Often to do with the use of lees (dead yeast), oak or malolactic conversion. In reds, you might ask for 'smooth' or 'silky' instead.

**Decant:** pour a wine into a decanter (or jug) to aerate it before drinking.

**Dry:** can refer to a taste, but can also describe wines with little residual sugar.

**Earthy:** solid descriptor for any wine that reminds you of – you guessed it – the earth (or its associated pals). Think: rocks, dust, pavements, plants, veggies and soil. If it reminds you of the ground somehow, it's earthy.

**Field blend:** a blend of grape varieties from the same vineyard.

**Finish:** the taste that lingers in your mouth post-swallow. (Even the cleaner version of that sentence sounds filthy, so let's lean in.)

**Fruity:** wine that's bursting with big fruit smells. For example, when you have a sniff of your wine and think 'Woof, that's a punch of red berry realness right there,' it's fruity.

**Lean:** textural term for wine that has good acidity, but isn't super fruity.

**Legs:** those clear streaks that wine can make on the side of your wineglass. Not that important. Can indicate amount of alcohol in the wine – big streak means more alc.

**Lift:** refreshing sensation that comes from acidity. Without lift, a wine can feel flabby and meh in your mouth.

**Magnum:** 1.5L bottle of wine

**Mouthfeel:** yeah, it's the way wine feels in your mouth. Usually refers to texture. Think: silken, complex or as rough as a cat's tongue.

**New World:** not European, basically. Usually refers to producers who label their wine by grape varietal rather than by **appellations** (see appellation in old World-y terms). So typically this refers to countries newer to the wine gambit like Australia, NZ, the US and South Africa. N.B. this term is not indicative of quality, just history.

**Noble grapes:** grapes with tiny crowns on them. Yeah nah, noble grapes are eighteen different international varieties of red and white grapes that span the flavour spectrum. Everything from Chenin Blanc to Cabernet Sauvignon, Sauvignon Blanc to Syrah. The most readily available varieties in the world.

**Non-vintage:** when several years of must are blended together. Usually in reference to Champagne.

**Oak:** whether it's from ageing in an oak barrel or in a steel vessel with oak chips floating about, oak is a choice way to add texture, aroma and flavour to wine. The most popular oaks are French, American and Hungarian/Eastern European.

**Oily:** textural term. Usually a full-bodied vino, leaving a viscousy feel in the mouth.

**Old World:** countries with winemaking traditions pre-15th century. Kids like Italy, France, Germany and the like.

**Opulent:** a textural description for a rich, bold, big-mama wine.

**Orange wine:** white wine treated like red – mucho skin contact and can be a bit sour.

**Pét-Nat:** short for Pétillant Naturel. Really smashable 'natural' sparkling wines that are super textured and similar in style to a cloudy cider or beer.

**Producer:** a winemaker who's also involved with growing the grapes. (Research has made me realise I had been using this term very wrongly for a very long time: a winemaker is not necessarily a producer if they're using someone else's fruit.)

**Reserve wine:** another cowboy term that's meant to indicate a winery's most premium releases.

**Silky:** the red wine equivalent of 'creamy'.

**Sommelier:** a trained wine professional who can be your spirit guide throughout a fine dining experience.

**Tannin:** naturally occurring compounds that come from the skins, stems and seeds of grapes.

**AMANDA** You'd recognise the tannin as a very dry sensation on your palate. Just say you've had a super strong cup of tea and you go 'Ooh, that's pretty hard'. That's what tannin is. The English discovered many, many years ago that if they threw milk into tea, it would smooth out the tannin. That's why we use oak in red wine. They generally have either a thicker skin or a higher anthocyanin count within the skin so you get a stronger perception of tannin and they use oak to help tame the tannin.

**Terroir:** the most adorable wine word because it's pronounced 'tare-wah' and makes me think of a snugly Loony Tunes character pronouncing 'Tara'. Terroir is a French term referring to the environment in which a wine is produced – everything from the climate and soil to the surrounding flora and fauna.

**Trellis:** the wires and posts that hold up the vines and keep 'em upright.

**Varietal:** a type of grape. Some people get funny when you say 'varietals' as plural, instead of 'varieties'. I don't have a strong opinion about this TBH. You do you. (For this book, we chose to refer to one variet*al* and many variet*ies*.)

**Velvety:** a textural term for wine that is oh so smooth and lush.

**Vintage:** the particular year in which the wine's grapes were harvested.

GLOSSARY

195

**Vintner:** another way of saying 'winemaker'.

**Winemaker:** come on, you know this. (Person who heads up the winemaking process. May or may not grow the grapes.)

**Yield:** the amount of grapes/vino a vineyard produces. Rule of thumb, the lower the yield, the more concentrated the wine.

# OLD WORLD-Y TERMS

**Appellation:** a region where certain grapes are grown and particular winemaking regulations are in play. France and Italy have the most famous bunch, for example, Anjou, Chablis, Champagne, Friuli-Venezia Giulia, Piedmont.

    In certain areas, 'appellation' is also applied to New World regions, for example, Calistoga, Stags Leap District, Oakville in Napa Valley AVA (American Viticultural Area). I could list more, but there are sixteen different appellations in Napa alone and I need to get lunch now.

**AoC (Appellation d'Origine Contrôlée):** a French classification system. Much like Italy's DOC, this guarantees the product comes from a certain region and holds to certain standards.

**Beaujolais cru:** wine that comes from one of the region's top ten vineyard sites.

**Château:** wine estates in Bordeaux that rock socks.

**Cru:** French word for 'growth'. In France, a Grand cru is pretty ooh la la. In Italy, a cru is a vineyard that's got a unique personality.

**Cuvée:** a blend of wine, espesh with sparklings.

**DOC (Denominazione di Origine Controllata):** an Italian classification system. Much like France's AoC, it refers to the wine's origins and what standards were upheld. DOCG (e Garantita) wines are meant to be superior to DOC wines.

**Domaine:** Burgundy's version of Bordeaux's 'château'.

**Grand cru:** 'great growth'. Kind of a complicated term though, as it varies from region to region as to whether it's referring to the top vineyards (Burgundy), wineries (Bordeaux) or village it comes from (Champagne).

GLOSSARY

197

**Premier cru:** also known as 'First Growth'. The wines and estates that are at the highest level in the Grand cru classification system in France, for example, Château Latour, Château Margaux and Château Haut-Brion.

**Qvevri:** ceramic vessels that were sealed with beeswax and/or stone and stored underground during fermentation.

# TECHNICAL/SCIENCEY TERMS

**Anthocyanins:** red pigments that occur in the skin of black/red grapes. Help contribute to the berry's astringent taste. You definitely don't need to remember this word.

**Barrel fermentation:** wine that's been fermented in barrels rather than stainless steel. Often has a more oaky quality, but it also affects the wine's texture and structure.

**Botrytis:** other term for 'noble rot' fungus. See noble rot.

**Brettanomyces:** a yeast with a Band-Aid aroma that can spoil a wine. Also known as Brett.

**Canopy management:** involves using a bunch of vineyard techniques to manage a grapevine's leaves, shoots and fruit. Done throughout winter, pruning all the way until harvest.

**Carbon dioxide:** the gas found in sparkling wine. Produced during fermentation.

**Carbonic maceration:** this will never come up in conversation. But just in case, it's a winemaking technique that's used a lot in Beaujolais and Languedoc-Roussillon. It produces fruity wines with soft tannins.

Chaptalisation: when winemakers add sugar to must before fermentation to pump up the wine's alcohol.

Clone: in this case, it's not an eerie AI character in the latest *Blade Runner* reboot. Commonly thought to be a cross-breeding of varieties (for example, Sauvignon Blanc + Cabernet Franc = Cabernet Sauvignon), it's actually when you take a vine with, say, naturally disease-resistant qualities or high yields and graft it onto another vine to create something same, same but better. Basically, it's a family of vines who were created by clonal selection from a big mama vine to get certain characteristics.

**Cooked:** when a wine has been stored in the sun or subject to extreme temperatures, making it lose its freshness.

**Corked/cork taint:** when a wine has been affected by wine cork taint. Can often smell like a pile of Nan's old newspapers are being hoarded in your bottle.

**Disgorgement:** ejecting grapey sediment from sparkling wine to ensure that the wine will be clear.

**Extended lees contact:** when lees have lengthy contact with the must, making the creamy effect of the lees more pronounced. Can last anywhere from months to years. See also lees.

**Fermentation:** how wine is made. Refers to the process of grape sugars converting into alcohol and carbon dioxide, with the help of old mate yeast.

**Filtration:** the process of filtering the wine to be more polished and maintain microbial stability within the bottle.

**Fining:** adding a protein or additive to remove astringency and clarify a wine.

**Isinglass:** ingredient made from fish bladders that is used to clarify wine. Clarify = make less cloudy.

**Lees:** dead yeast cells that can add a creamy texture to the palate. See also **Extended lees contact**.

**Malolactic fermentation:** the reason for dat creamy, buttery flavour in your Chardy. It's that clever little winemaking process of chemically converting sharp malic acid into softer lactic acid. Involves Oenoccocus Oeni bacteria.

**Must:** what you get when you crush a bunch o' grapes. Includes all the juice and pulp of the stems, skins and seeds. Midway between juice and wine.

**Night harvesting:** harvesting grapes at night in order to keep the fruit cool and maintain better control over the fermentation process.

**Noble rot:** also known as Botrytis Cinerea. It's a grey mould that can be used purposefully to enhance a vino's sweetness and flavour, for example, in Riesling and Tokay.

**Oenology:** study and science of winemaking. Not same diff as viticulture.

**Oxidation:** a bloody nightmare for your wine. A little oxygen is great to open up your wine, but too much will make the flavours and aromas dissipate and replace them with a vinegary mess. Think of it like a cut apple going brown. Iz no good and considered a fault.

**Phenolic grip/Tannic grip:** phenols are the wee chemical compounds that affect the taste, colour and texture of wine. Phenols come from the skin, seeds and stems of grapes and are most present in red grapes. When peeps are talking about phenolic/tannic grip, they're talking about the loud texture of the wine, the feeling that the wine is gripping onto your taste buds for dear life.

**Phylloxera:** the yellow aphids that made Europe (and the rest of the winemaking world) its bish in the 1860s. Still an issue for winemakers as they spread super easily – they ride people's shoes like they're giant ponies. Most effective cure for these aphids is ripping up the vines and replanting with Native American rootstock + grafting.

**PPM:** parts per million, innit.

**Punch-down:** manually pushing down cheeky grape skins into the must when they've risen to the top inside the fermentation tank.

**Racking:** to siphon wine off from one container to the next, leaving sediment behind.

**Residual sugar:** those natural sugars that weren't converted into alcohol during the fermentation process. Actually less sweet than added sugar.

**Riddling:** otherwise known as 'remuage'. Rotating (near) upside down wine bottles clockwise and anti-clockwise to help sediment collect at the neck (just in time for disgorgement). Common with champagne.

**Secondary fermentation:** type a) how sparkling wine gets so sparkly. Type b) when still wine gets a bit bubbly. Not in the fun way.

**Sediment:** that shizz at the bottom of your wine bottle. Usually a mish-mash of skins, seeds and yeasts.

**Skin contact:** when white wines are smooshed with their skins still on. Red wines notoriously ferment with their clothes on, so the term usually pops up when talking about orange wines. Depending on the winemaker, the length of skin contact can range from a couple of hours to a few days.

**Sulphites/sulphur dioxide:** a common preservative used to kill bill bacteria and combat oxidisation. Super effective fungicide against powdery mildew. Easy to confuse with sulphites, which are naturally occurring chemicals created throughout the fermentation process.

**Tartaric acid:** the most common form of acid in grapes and wine. (Malic acid is the other principal acid in grapes.)

**TCA:** the compound largely responsible for cork taint. Stands for 'tricholoroanisole'.

GLOSSARY

**Viticulture:** study of grape-growing. Not same diff as oenology.

**Vitis vinifera:** means 'a vine of wine-bearing grapes'. The most common type of vines for cultivating wine, though nearly all of them got wiped out in the 1860s by phylloxera. Produces varieties like Cab Sav, Chardonnay, Pinot Noir. Basically all the ones you know and love. Non-vitis vinifera include native American varieties like Concord and Scuppernong, and hybrids like Muller-Thurgau and Baco Noir.

**Volatile acidity:** acetic acid that gives wine a vinegary taste.

**Yeast:** what a banger term to end on. The tiny fungi that convert grape sugars into alcohol. Can occur naturally in a vineyard, known as wild or spontaneous fermentation. The more predictable yeasts are cultured yeasts, made from specifically selected little guys.

# ACKNOWLEDGEMENTS

First up, I want to acknowledge what a (white) privilege it has been to write this book. The majority of *Everything Happens for a Riesling* was written in Melbourne on Wurundjeri land, part of the Kulin nation. I pay my respects to Elders past, present and emerging and recognise that this creative venture is but a blip in the long tradition of creativity established here by the oldest living culture in the world, the First Nations of Australia.

Researching extensively about Australia's geography, and wine's history with colonisation, has forced me to reflect on how we have treated (and still treat) the traditional owners of this land. So, even though this is a largely apolitical book, I think it's worth acknowledging that, at the time of writing, our government blocked a proposal for a constitutionally enshrined First Nations voice, as modestly requested in the historic Uluru Statement from the Heart. The Uluru Statement is an unprecedented First Nations consensus on how Aboriginal people in this nation want to be constitutionally recognised. Lessbehonest, it's embarrassing to think we still don't have meaningful Indigenous recognition in the 21st century and that non-Indigenous people (myself included) haven't been better allies. It's time we all stepped up to ensure the Uluru Statement is acted upon, so we can make a better Australia. Special thanks to Dr Shireen Morris for her consultation over Indigenous constitutional reform. (I can't wait to read your book, *Radical Heart!*)

I also want to acknowledge everyone who worked hard to bring this weird and wonderful book to life. Even though you are all at the top of your field and incredibly busy folk, you were very generous with your time and talent. Thank you for letting me ask (and re-ask) a lot of basic questions and for being so approachable. HUGE thanks to

Amanda Yallop, Tim Watkins, Ben Law, Rosie Waterland,
Becky Durham, Sam Connew, Mikey Ellis, Michael Ng, Imogen Diks,
my mum, sister and brother-in-law, my wine club as well as all my
mates who supported me throughout this overwrought writing process.

*Everything Happens for a Riesling* would not exist without my
unflappable editor, Lex Hirst. Thank you for your vision, sense of
humour and for knowing when I could push things further (and pull
my head in). This has been a dream project and you are a dreamboat.

Thank you to the rest of the extraordinary team at Penguin
Random House, in particular Adam Laszczuk, Meredith Curnow
and Genevieve Buzo.

Thank you to illustrator Cath Glassby for investing so much
of your creativity into this. I love the worlds you create and appreciate
how beautiful you've made this book.

Special shout-out to Chance The Rapper for the banger that is
'All Night'. This song was my backing track while I wrote and really
helped keep the tone fun and upbeat.

And lastly, thank you to those of you who bought this book
with cold hard cash. I really hope this has been a welcoming intro
to the world of wine and that you've had a laugh while reading it.
Wine is such a gorgeous time capsule and expression of place, so my
hope is that this book gives you permission to capture more precious
(and delicious) moments with your family and friends. Have fun on
your wine adventures.

Cheers, GRACE X